ON DIRECTING SHAKESPEARE

ON DIRECTING
SHAKESPEARE

Interviews with Contemporary Directors

RALPH BERRY

CROOM HELM LONDON

BARNES & NOBLE BOOKS NEW YORK

(a division of Harper & Row Publishers, Inc.)

Printed and bound in Great Britain by
REDWOOD BURN LIMITED
Trowbridge & Esher

CONTENTS

To all who helped

PREFACE

This book has its origins in a letter which appeared in *The Times* of London on 13 October 1971. In the controversy that followed Peter Brook's brilliant and astonishing *A Midsummer Night's Dream*, Jonathan Miller wrote:

> Mandarin bardolatry is on the move again, I see. Your correspondents who attack Peter Brook's *Dream* have systematically misconceived the task of the theatrical director and by implication, therefore, have failed to understand the relationship that exists between tradition and the individual talent. According to them the director should modestly efface his own personality and allow the text to speak for itself.
>
> One might sympathize with this dogma if the text in question contained, in addition to the speeches that comprise it, additional clues which specified the sort of diction that would count. Given the fact that Shakespeare left no collateral instructions it is hard to imagine how one would ever know that one was in the presence of a version wherein the text was speaking for itself. How would the characters speak in such a performance? What accents would they use and where would the proper emphases fall? How would the cast stand and what would they all be dressed in? What does a fairy look like and in what way do his utterances differ from those of ordinary mortals?
>
> Even if the author were alive to tell us it seems doubtful whether he would be able to give a satisfactory answer to all these questions. And even if he were able to stand up and object to certain interpretations of his own text it seems quite likely from what one knows of living authors that he might be pleasantly surprised by other equally startling departures from the orthodox version.
>
> The mystery of Shakespeare's genius lies in the fact that innumerable performances of his plays can be rendered, few of which are closely compatible with one another, most of which, however, are at least congruent with the speeches as written. Since we can never know which one of these corresponds with Shakespeare's original intention the director must satisfy himself with the task of trying to improvise a set of people who could all convincingly mean

something by the speeches assigned to them. In order to do this he may put the play into a new period and even set it in an entirely novel circumstance.

The point is that the act of dramatic interpretation consists of a journey backwards through time in the effort to find some significant historical ground upon which to raise an eloquent representation of human conflict. Success is then rated, not by the degree to which the performance approximates to an entirely unknowable state of Shakespeare's mind, but by the extent to which the text now speaks with more or less coherent vitality. It may be that this elusive vitality is best arrived at by setting the plays in the author's own period or possibly in the period from which he took the original story.

However, if one is going to be consistent about this and not merely lapse into a mock Tudor antiquarianism, it will soon become apparent that elements will have been introduced which will almost certainly strike the modern audience as esoteric gimmicks. What was a fairy to the Elizabethan audience? Surely not the gauzy Pre-Raphaelite creatures of yesteryear. Few of us believe in fairies now and yet there *is* something intriguing about the concept of a supernatural world that lies beyond the reach of common sense.

Brook, I think, found, to many people's satisfaction, an objective correlative of this notion which, while it may have violated Shakespeare's unstated thought upon the matter, fulfilled a version of what he did actually write down.

We accept without question the successive transformations of scripture throughout the history of painting and see nothing odd, vain or arrogant in a painter who sets his Annunciation in a mediaeval Flemish town. Shakespeare himself wrought the same changes upon antiquity, not because he arrogantly supposed their stories to be smaller or thinner than his own imagination but because he realized that one of the tasks of art is to overthrow the tyranny of time and to recreate a universe within which the dead converse at ease with the living.

With the passage of time Shakespeare's plays have quite properly assumed the status of myths and it is the honourable fate of all great myths to suffer imaginative distortions at the hands of those to whom they continue to give consolation and nourishment. The story of Oedipus existed before Sophocles changed it again and when Freud incorporated the tale into his theory of family conflict he was merely adding another substantial chapter to a tale whose telling can never be finished. So let it be with Shakespeare.

I found this an eloquent and striking statement of the licence a director demands for his art. In his insistence on the priority of the text, with all its vitality, over 'Shakespeare', Miller placed matters in a perspective fresh to me. It was at once clear that his letter demolishes many spurious criticisms of modern directorial methods. But other, more reasoned, questions remained. I resolved to know more about these matters, which I had previously encountered largely as a member of the audience in Shakespearian productions. And so I conceived the idea of interviewing a small group of leading directors, in England, the Continent and America with the aim of investigating their approach to Shakespeare and their salient methods in producing him. Together, these men would, I hoped, create a unique collective answer to the question, 'What *is* Shakespeare today?' This is the record of that investigation.

These interviews compose, in effect, an extended conversation about Shakespeare in the theatre today. There are recurring themes, but I did not seek to impose an oral questionnaire upon the pattern of encounter. The interests of each director guided the movement of conversation. Certain questions which I put to some would have been irrelevant to others, or at least implicitly answered elsewhere. And there are, natural-ly, a great many questions which I did not ask. A successful director is by definition an exceptionally active man, and I did not seek to prolong discussion of any issue beyond a point which might strain the courtesy of my hosts. Moreover, I was not bent on a work of stage history: so I ruthlessly suppressed any inclination to ask questions on the marginalia of productions, on the lines of 'did you double the Ghost and First Grave-digger?' The allusions here to any given production are illustrative of a directorial approach to Shakespeare. They are not, in themselves, the subject of investigation. The prime aim is an increased understanding of the relations between Shakespeare, today's theatre, and ourselves.

I acknowledge with pleasure the generous support given to this project by the Canada Council, and by the University of Manitoba. My greatest debt, however, is to the directors whose unfailing courtesy has made it possible, and I record my deep appreciation of their co-operation. They have provided, and will provide, a heightened sense of the critique of contemporaneity that Shakespeare always represents.

INTRODUCTION

The problems of discourse commonly arise from a word which is used in diverse senses. Such a word is 'Shakespeare'. Two main senses are discernible in discussion. They overlap, naturally, but I believe that most people give an underlying emphasis to their use of the term. 'Shakespeare' is in the first place a man, a classic author: one has an image of a face, a beard, an expression. In the second place, 'Shakespeare' is shorthand for the works of Shakespeare: one recognises a bound volume, play-texts, the foundations of a production. Certain consequences flow immediately from one's election of the prior sense. If a man, Shakespeare has, it is felt, some rights over his plays and us. He is the greatest English writer, and the greatest play-wright of whom the world has record. We owe him our devotion, and in preserving and re-performing his plays we serve him. Such an atti-tude escapes into the realm of aesthetic theory, and insists that the intention of the author be of prime account in the interpretation and presentation of his works. But if Shakespeare is purely a text, then different considerations apply. We do not serve a man, we excavate or exploit a quarry. The plays cease to be expressions of intention, or attempts at communication; rather, they become material. Whether or not we make open use of Cocteau's provocative 'textes-prétextes', the term he applied to his Shakespearian productions, we accept that the umbilical cord linking the man and work is severed. I exaggerate these attitudes to make their import plain; most people do not approach the matter with this kind of logical finality, and traces of the alternative attitude are doubtless present in even the extreme pro-ponents of one or other. The most dedicated servitor of Shakespeare will readily concede that he built multiple meanings into his texts, and the most ruthless practitioner of the quarry-text school may yet feel that he is accomplishing a higher intention, a willed meaning, of Shakespeare. Still, for practical purposes, the conflict is there. One can simply choose sides, if one wishes, and leave it there. But the conflict is so perennially fascinating, the issues so broad and subtle, that one should surely wish to investigate further. To choose sides too early is to evade the challenge.

Let us take the assertion (as it is often phrased) that directors should permit the text 'to speak for itself'. That is impossible. To begin

with, the text itself is a massive variable. For half the plays of Shakespeare, our sole source is the Folio, published seven years after his
death and seen through the press by his literary executors. The
remaining plays exist additionally in single play-text (quarto) versions,
a number of which are evidently corrupt and highly untrustworthy.
Often the better quartos are at variance with the Folio, and we cannot
be sure that Folio represents Shakespeare's final thoughts. Standards
of type-setting and proof-reading bear little relation to those of the
present day, and we have no original to check: saving a fragment of
Sir Thomas More, no manuscript in Shakespeare's hand survives. It is
agreed that there are numerous corrupt and dubious passages in even
the best-preserved of the plays we have. Then, the texts are by modern
standards starved of stage-directions. These directions are usually
limited to straightforward details of entrances and exits, and factual
statements of non-verbal actions: *Throws him a purse*, and so on.
There is nothing at all corresponding to the interpretative annotations
with which a contemporary dramatist will interlard his dialogue. What
we have are the words, and the major actions: no more. And this is
only the beginning, for the texts that we have cannot, in many instances, be presented in their complete versions. It is a question of
length. There is no particular reason why *The Comedy of Errors* or
Twelfth Night should not be played in their entirety. But *Hamlet*, in
a conflation of the second Quarto and the Folio texts, would last over
five hours. Much the same applies to *King Lear, Troilus and Cressida,
Antony and Cleopatra*, and others. Whatever the playing time
audiences were accustomed to, whatever the speed of performance,
these texts have always been cut heavily and always will be. How, then,
does one cut? The playing version that the director selects bears
always the imprint of his own mind. There is no way of making a
neutral cut. One can try to arrive at a 'skeletal' play, the residue
corresponding, if one likes, to Shakespeare's extended stage-instructions;
but there is no certain means of identifying this playing version.
Tradition is no sure guide. The Polonius-Reynaldo scene in *Hamlet*
(II, i) is usually cut, but a director is perfectly at liberty to argue that
it throws indispensable light on the play. No scene in *Antony and
Cleopatra* is more easily spared than the Ventidius-Silius dialogue (III,
i), yet its *Realpolitik* is a fundamental perspective on Antony. In sum,
a Shakespeare production in its simplest formulation — the words and
actions presented to the public — must be governed at many points by
the decision of the director. There is no other authority to appeal to.

All this is obvious enough. The real problems now begin to emerge, for the words of the text as chosen have to be delivered by actors who have certain physical characteristics, who are apparelled in a certain way, who speak their lines with a certain emphasis. *Meaning*, broadly, is the product of what the audience perceives as emerging from these immensely complex events. And there is no escaping the responsibility for directing, i.e. determining these events. Jonathan Miller's question goes to the heart of the matter: 'What does a fairy look like?'

What, indeed? Most of us, I suppose, would, if appealed to, conjure up an image of the children's book illustrations on which we were brought up. It is unnecessary to argue in detail how potentially misleading this must be. In visualising a style of illustration, we assume a reality of connection. We see, perhaps, a visual contemporary of Shepard's *Wind in the Willows* or Beatrix Potter. These matters are rooted in the culture of every nation, and must surely be well removed from the reality that 'fairy' connoted to the Elizabethans. There is no question of a 'correct' translation of fairy for modern audiences: the imaginative leap has to be made by each director. Peter Hall, for instance, brought into being a group of earth-stained urchins. But we cannot expect 'fairy' to accomplish the task of effortlessly defining itself for us.

Words, in fact, are the critical obstacles that the modern interpreter of Shakespeare has to overcome. The problem is paradoxically more exacting for the British and Americans than for any other nation. The reader who is formally engaged in translating Shakespeare into a foreign tongue gives each word a special consideration. The normal Anglo-American reader assumes that he is perfectly familiar with the mass of Shakespearian vocabulary. He therefore retains his energies for the difficult or obscure terms. He looks up 'provulgate' or 'hugger-mugger', and finds out what centuries of scholarly labour have made available. He does not look up 'court', or 'honour', or 'art' — indeed, there is nothing to look up. But these are precisely the trap-words, the words that we retain with similar meanings but which rest on assumptions and attitudes that have long grown obsolete or changed radically.

'Court' will make the point as forcefully as any term. As Konrad Swinarski explains, his productions of *All's Well That Ends Well* and *A Midsummer Night's Dream* rest on a central conception of 'Court'. It is the grand image of Shakespeare, for him. Now, for the average Anglo-American of our day, 'Court' is purely a decorative appendage to the political and social life of the capital. Its doings are as chronicled

in the Court Circular, and take up a little daily space in *The Times* and
Daily Telegraph. The Elizabethan sense of 'Court' as the centre of
power in the land is now scarcely accessible to us. With an exercise
of the historical imagination, we can appreciate that the court in
Hamlet is a dangerous and politically charged milieu, with its quota of
careerists, ministers and executive power. We will normally fail to
realise that 'Court' in this sense has any relevance to the comedies.
But the Elizabethan recognition of 'Court' as the Government, the one
place where all the great careers were to be made, could scarcely have
been neutralised simply because they were watching a Pleasant
Comedy. The resonances are there in the text, waiting to be sounded.
Swinarski's perception that *Court* is *Government* is a central reminder
of the difficulty with words, that they imply questions and issues yet
permit evasion. Words become a formula for divesting events of their
meaning.

The director has to re-create meaning, to re-activate the decaying,
amorphous words of the text. He is not an historical scholar (though he
must be in touch with the discoveries of scholarship), and he is not a
restorer. His task is to identify for his day the vital elements in a text,
and to communicate them. Every production of Shakespeare pre-
supposes a national group which is the predominant audience. (Of
course, a summer production in Stratford may play to a largely
international audience, but my essential point remains.) The meanings
latent in the text have to be actualised with that audience in mind.
A Coriolanus founded on the overtones of an English public school
upbringing is a perfectly valid conception, for an English audience.
To an audience unfamiliar with English ways these particular meanings would fail to resonate; but there are always alternatives. The
militaristic side of Coriolanus' upbringing finds echoes in the social
structure of many nations and tribes, but happens not to be a strong
English tradition. Even so simple a term as 'soldier' needs a specific
(and not a generalised) audience before it can be satisfactorily
defined. (Consider what 'soldier' connotes to a Japanese, a Swede, a
German, an American.) The point is that meanings are not lexical
absolutes, to be animated by the players. Meanings are generated by
community and history; the audience participates in and establishes
them. The audience does not, as it were, blankly spectate at a set of
visual and aural images. Thus the director has to enter into that
audience's bloodstream, to be aware of the images that compose the
present and the past of the community — its felt history, that is to say.
But this leads us to the decisions that a director takes in presenting a

play of Shakespeare.

The director makes three cardinal decisions in presenting a play of Shakespeare. He chooses the play: he determines the playing text: he creates the metaphoric vehicle for the production, the ambience generated by setting and costume. I came to believe in the course of this enquiry that the most important decision is the first. Its significance is normally obscured by the sheer mechanics of mounting a production. Much of the Shakespeare we see is put on in a festival or repertory theatre, and the choice of play is circumscribed, often determined, by factors of cost, actor availability, the need to ensure heavy box-office activity, and so on. In these circumstances the nominal canon of thirty-seven or thirty-eight plays can sometimes shrink to *Hamlet* and *Twelfth Night*. Michael Kahn, Trevor Nunn and Robin Phillips have much to say on these matters, which should be sympathetically received. But I point to the occasions where a leading director, of established reputation, has virtually a free hand to select his play. And now the choice becomes all-important, for he will not select a text until he senses its mysterious affinities with the movement of the times. While he has no doubt an active and personal engagement with a play, he has additionally the sense that certain chords in it can be made to vibrate with a peculiar intensity in the contemporary mind. To vary the figure, the director becomes the barometer of society.

Let us illustrate. The most dangerous, the most politically vibrant play in the canon was once *Richard II*. That is because it deals with a deposition. It is on record that a performance of *Richard II* was staged, at the instigation of Essex's followers, as a direct preliminary to an attempted *coup d'état*. 'I am Richard the Second, know ye not that?' said the old Queen to Lambarde. But today nobody regards the play as an anti-monarchic manifesto. It has become an existentialist analysis of a human being stripped of his exterior appurtenances, reduced to the ultimate problem of defining himself. The 'meaning' — the thrust of the play — has changed radically. Other plays come and go with the flux of politics: *Julius Caesar* and *Coriolanus* periodically supply analogues with dictatorship and class conflict. (A version of *Coriolanus*, Dennis's *The Invader of his Country*, once supplied a topical commentary on the Old Pretender.) Some plays have simply had to wait for their audiences. *Troilus and Cressida* (with *Measure for Measure*) is now one of *the* plays for our times — almost all the directors whom I conversed with expressed a special interest in it — yet until a generation ago it had virtually no stage history whatever. It is too early to say so with confidence, but perhaps *Timon of Athens* will come into this category;

it is certainly possible that Peter Brook's production at the Bouffes-du-Nord (October 1974) will herald a wave of interest. The history of Shakespeare on the stage is full of instances where plays, neglected for years, have suddenly been re-established as centres of contemporary interest. But on the whole, the most fascinating exercise of the director's barometric function lies in his choice of a play that is already popular. He then displays a facet of the text that has not been properly understood, and he demonstrates that *this* is the play for today.

Thus, the *Henry V* of a generation ago was a strongly nationalist statement, classically formulated in the Olivier film. This remained true for a number of years after the war. The Royal Shakespeare Company's production of the mid-sixties demonstrated — what is indeed true — that the text contains a latent anti-war statement, and this version was given full weight. It is now, as I guess, the orthodox view of the play. One need not labour the point that what was possible in 1964 was impossible in 1944: and vice versa. The text does not change, audiences do. Or again, the Peter Hall/David Warner *Hamlet* of the same period showed him as a student. This, oddly enough, is what the text actually declares Hamlet to be. But the image of Hamlet as an apathetic, alienated graduate student provoked considerable reaction from those accustomed to the Renaissance prince. The younger generation took very much to *their* Hamlet. Here a production crystallised a generational division, a further movement of the times. And finally, there is the rigorously post-colonial *Tempest* of Jonathan Miller. This view indisputably reflects a real concern of the text, yet until very recently nobody *knew* what decolonisation was like; it had never happened. The production, and its audience, had to wait for the events of the 1950s and 1960s. It is, then, a complete naïveté to speak of the 'meaning' of a Shakespeare play as an entity that can be defined, established, and placed on record in perpetuity. The play is changed by the act of selection, which implies the social context of the new production. In selecting the play, the director undertakes to guide his audience to an area of contemporary consciousness, and enlarge its understanding.

The choice of play should be recognised for the paramount act that it is. In every way, this act governs the next decision, the determination of the playing text. This is not, I think, a matter on which one can usefully generalise. The plays themselves are so diverse in nature, and we ought to accept Peter Brook's distinction between the plays which are very elaborately written and those which are very tightly organised.

The Brook *Midsummer Night's Dream* was based on an uncut text; Trevor Nunn has never directed an uncut Shakespeare. Miller cuts freely, Swinarski most unwillingly. Kahn cuts less and less. Practice is extremely various. We should however identify the nature of cutting. Essentially it is an affair of cutting the crystal, of presenting an object so as to reflect light at the desired angles. If, for instance, Shylock's soliloquy of I, iii, 42-53 is cut ('How like a fawning publican he looks! I hate him for he is a Christian . . .'), together with Jessica's testimony that he had often sworn he would rather have Antonio's flesh than twenty times the money, the effect of this is to reduce sharply the element of predetermined hatred in Shylock's attitudes, and throw the weight of his later conduct on to the disaster of his daughter's flight with a Christian. These cuts neither mutilate the text nor go against its grain, but they do prepare the way for a more sympathetic treatment of Shylock allied to an ironic and sceptical view of the Venetians. And this strategy, naturally, is related to the prior decision of play selection. Broadly, a contemporary audience is well able to see the scales adjusted more in favour of Shylock than past audiences; it is a central possibility in the text that Shakespeare's infallible tact has left open. Cutting, then, should emphasise a certain quality, a certain source of vitality, in the full original. This is not to deny that cutting can be brutal, capricious, insensitive. Its function is none the less to illuminate, and not lay waste, the original text.

It has to be added that cuts of a certain magnitude are necessarily a phase in adapting, even rewriting, the original text. One can scarcely hope to mount the three parts of *Henry VI* in their entirety. So one solution, as in John Barton's version for the Royal Shakespeare Company, is to reduce three plays to the length of two. This requires some rewriting of transitional passages and expository material. A talent at least for pastiche is indispensable here. Beyond that lies the full-scale adaptation, as in Giorgio Strehler's massive *Das Spiel der Mächtigen*, which is formally announced as 'by Giorgio Strehler after Shakespeare's *Henry VI*'. Evidently such productions extend the history of Shakespearian adaptations, which is more enduring than is generally realised. (Shaw, for example, was brought up on Colley Cibber's version of *Richard III*.) I know of no general criteria for judging such adaptations: each one is a separate enterprise, and will be judged on the skill and tact with which the adaptor interprets and re-animates the vital essences of the original text. The Barton *Wars of the Roses* was widely acclaimed, yet the same author's recent version of *King John* has been as widely criticised. Strehler's *Das Spiel der Mächtigen* has had a prolonged success. On a smaller scale, Trevor Nunn admits to enjoying writing a line or two himself (for good technical reasons) and is positive that no one ever notices. Practice, clearly, is extremely diverse and wide-ranging in its expedients. It seems best to regard cutting as one side of a coin, on the obverse side of which is rewriting and adapting.

The stage setting and costumes comprise the metaphoric vehicle, or ambience, of the production. In the mode of choice which the director makes here his entire philosophy of production will be revealed. On no issue did I encounter a greater diversity of opinion. While the categories are not watertight, the major possibilities open to the director are Renaissance: modern: a historical setting that is neither Renaissance nor modern: abstract-eclectic. Each has its rationale.

(i) *Renaissance*

The immediate possibility for most of Shakespeare's plays: to it can be added mediaeval, for the histories, and Roman, for the Roman plays. The central idea is that the period of composition, or the period to which the author alludes, should be directly reflected in the costumes and settings. These in turn will reflect the language, the concerns, and the assumptions of the text. This strategy has more resources than its apparently simple literalism would indicate. Negatively, it avoids virtually all problems of anachronism. (If a character refers to doublet and hose, that is what he is wearing. Malvolio's cross-gartering requires no translation.) It marries easily with a version of the Elizabethan stage, if that is the setting the director wishes. Unlike contemporary styles, it denies nothing in the text. It is powerfully retentive of meanings. Moreover, the policy need not be dogmatically historical-literal: it can tolerate *pourparlers* with eclecticism. The recent *Julius Caesar* at the Royal Shakespeare Company was staged in Roman costume, but in black leather (which is quite un-Roman) suggesting strongly the aura of Fascism. The Renaissance approach has distinguished advocates: Peter Hall, for one, has always preferred it, and his baroque *Tempest* has recently displayed facets of the text available only to a Renaissance production. Swinarski found Polish Renaissance settings perfectly suitable for his productions. Kahn prefers to choose between Renaissance and modern. The simple, powerful strategy of the historical approach is never likely to be discredited.

(ii) *Modern*

The logic of Shakespeare flows easily into other channels, and the contemporary setting is the most obvious of them. If Shakespeare is our contemporary, the argument runs, let him be presented in the costume of the present day. And indeed this brusque attack upon the relevance of a text is virtually guaranteed positive results. It immediately breaks through the mental barrier existing for many between (say) kings, queens and consuls and the present day, and appears to establish the authenticity of the production's credentials. Those knowing the text well, for whom the mental barrier is no problem, will none the less be engaged and gripped by each piece of modern translation that the director introduces. The approach undoubtedly communicates rapidly and directly to a large portion of the audience. Against this are some losses. A part of the original text will make no sense at all. References to swords, horses, clothes and so on must be cut, ignored, or left in as a distracting presence. Much has to be denied in the text to shape up the present-day analogies: and this denial may be altogether too sweeping. Shakespeare, in Patrick Cruttwell's phrase, is *not* our contemporary, and in seeking to establish the converse proposition one can damage irrevocably the fabric of the text, which is sustained by a web of assumptions and attitudes confined to Renaissance thinking. And this in spite of the genuinely illuminating analogues that a modern setting, always prolific of stage invention, can supply. I recall a *Love's Labour's Lost* which opened with a group of students dreamily passing a marijuana pipe around. This is not a bad analogue to the state of fantasy into which the Navarrese courtiers are sunk, a state destined to be challenged and refuted by the realities of the later stages. Still, this invention evidently fails to grip (say) the concept of 'fame', or for that matter the known unwillingness of students to banish women from their academies. The danger is always that an immediate point can be made vividly and tellingly, but that it relies on a set of assumptions about our own society that the remainder of the text cannot sustain. There is a direct and irreconcilable conflict between the text and an overt, physicalised translation into modernity. On the whole, the approach seems best adapted to the comedies, where the gains usually outweigh the losses. The mode is out of favour for staging the trage-dies, and indeed there is something curiously dated about the phrase 'modern dress *Hamlet*'. But there is always the chance that current events will supply a set of analogues so compelling that the director can accept the invitation to make open use of them.

(iii) *Historical*

And this is the rationale for the choice of an historical setting other than the present, or Renaissance/mediaeval/Roman. Logically there is little real difference between (ii) and (iii). In practice, this species of historical period-analogue has great resources, simply because the field of choice is so enormous. We need, however, to keep in mind the distinction that Michael Kahn draws between '*décor*' and 'concept'. By '*décor*' he means a period style that is chosen for its visual elegance, and offers a purely cosmetic way of dressing up the text. 'Concept' means that in pointing to a particular set of national and historical circumstances via the costumes, the director marks close and striking affinities with the realities of the text. A production based on period analogy must be judged on its orientation to *décor* or concept; but these are not exclusive categories. They are best thought of as composing a spectrum.

Beginning at the *décor* end of the spectrum, I instance a *Love's Labour's Lost* patterned visually upon *Les Très Riches Heures du Duc de Berri*. Elegant and appealing, the costumes contributed primarily a mood, an aura. It is hard to detect more than the broadest of analogies between the courts of Navarre and the Duc de Berri. The production was in fact innocent of genuine reflection upon the text. That is not a criticism but a statement of category: the production had modest aims and accomplished them successfully. Or take Kahn's Risorgimento *Romeo and Juliet*, for which naturally he has an entirely realistic appraisal: the setting remains Italian, is congruent with the feuds of the period, and supplies many possibilities of display and invention. That is sufficient, and requires no defence. But the more ambitious enterprises seek always to turn local visual opportunities to conceptual advantage. Not infrequently, a Shakespeare comedy is set in the early nineteenth century. Now the advantage of this is that the lovers can take on the mode of Romantic posturing. The strategy works well for *Twelfth Night* and *The Two Gentlemen of Verona*, where Orsino and Valentine can be got up to look like Byronic heroes. This broad allusion to the cult of Byron genuinely expresses a reality of the text — Orsino and Valentine are both *poseurs* — and the costumes help to *explain* the play, as well as dress it.

Peter Brook's Watteau *Love's Labour's Lost* rests not on a few well-taken opportunities, but on a central conception: that the world of Watteau is the ideal visual analogue to the world of Navarre. The Watteau *fête champêtre* comprehends, if you like, anti-festive forces, and these forces are symbolised in the alienated figure, who may be

Watteau, present in the painting. This corresponds with Mercade, and
all he stands for. 'The words of Mercury are harsh after the songs of
Apollo.' (Shakespeare surely means the collocation of Mercade-
Mercury to reverberate.) Thus the production, though of course highly
decorative, is not *décor*. It is an act of criticism of a very high order.

All period analogies, of the non-decorative order, are acts of
criticism. When they succeed, they impose a permanent layer over the
text in the minds of the audience. Tyrone Guthrie translated *Troilus
and Cressida* into the Europe of the early twentieth century: the
Trojans, English officers of the Household Cavalry; the Greeks, Kaiser
Wilhelm's Germans. At one level, this concept covered a number of
finely taken opportunities: Ulysses, Admiral Tirpitz; Helen, an
Edwardian chorus girl married into the peerage, beautifully embodying
the triviality that Shakespeare depicts in the nominal *casus belli*;
Thersites, a war correspondent setting up his box camera and tripod.
The voyeurism of Pandarus and homosexuality of Achilles translated
easily into the idiom of the period. But more profoundly, Guthrie
caught a sense of two societies in conflict, two nations locked in a war
of values and attrition, and this in a period near enough to be
poignant but not conveying the fatal dissonances of a contemporary
war. Proximity can numb thought and stifle reactions. The Trojan war
may be the poetic archetype of all wars, but in the minds of the
audience all wars are not equal: 1914-18 is not the War of the Spanish
Succession, nor is it Vietnam. Guthrie's immense theatrical flair pro-
pounded an insidiously suggestive vehicle for the thoughts and
emotions of his audience.

Clearly, we are contemplating the fact that audiences have memories
as well as sensory apparatuses. History happens, and it changes people,
partly because history is recorded and remembered. A Shakespeare
production is totally within its rights in basing itself upon this central
fact, and appealing to an audience's knowledge of what has happened.
Take Jonathan Miller's *Measure for Measure*. This exploits what is in
effect a pun of history, that the city of Duke Vincentio is also the city
of Freud. The pun would be meaningless, but for the play's unquestion-
able concern with sexual repression. Thus Miller, in setting his production in the Vienna of the 1930s, was able to throw a brilliant light upon
a certain area of the text. And in this, he appealed to an ineluctable
fact for today's audiences: we cannot un-know Freud. Robin Phillips'
Measure for Measure, also of 1975, made the same point. Set in the
Vienna of 1912, his production identified sexual repression as the core
of the play. To this was added a distinctively 1975 awareness of

corruption in high places, and the feminist issue of Isabella's integrity (and not, as such, 'chastity'). The production was structured around the audience's sense of past and contemporary history.

A consequence of this approach is that strong light implies shadow, that certain aspects of the text can expect at best a neutral exposition. I do not think this a major drawback. The fact is that a Shakespeare text is so large, and comprehends so many possibilities, that a metaphor which illuminates a single major aspect within the two hours of playing time is fully self-justified. What is certainly desirable is that the director, in advancing his metaphor, should not make it so rigidly schematic as to exclude all unwanted meanings. The best directors will always play for additional meanings, for ambivalences and possibilities that go beyond the main outline of the structure. The suggestion can be stronger than the statement. Still, it is undeniable that separate metaphors can coexist peacefully within the same text. The Miller post-colonial *Tempest* and the Hall baroque *Tempest* are incompatible with each other, but perfectly congruent with the text: and that is all that matters.

The extreme of the *decor*-concept spectrum is, I suggest, occupied by history. Not a specific historical period, but history itself. This is territory claimed if not owned by the Marxists: the idea is that Shakespeare depicts a dialectic of historical forces that is unfolding to our present day. Really, this idea is a modern development of Samuel Johnson's view that characters in Shakespeare are not individuals, but species. Thus they are representative of social groups, or classes, in conflict. Naturally, this approach works best for *Coriolanus*, for Marxists the premier play in the canon. (Not, I think, since the 'Stavisky' *Coriolanus* in the Paris of 1933 has anyone presented *Coriolanus* as a *right*-wing play.) Other plays emerge well from the Marxist treatment though. If one views *The Merchant of Venice* as based on the critique of capitalism focused in the Antonio-Shylock debate of I, iii, then the whole drama can logically be developed as an ironic scrutiny of Venetian values. What, after all, is Antonio's position but the absurd claim that overseas investment is morally superior to taking straight interest on capital? (And this at a point in history when mediaeval denunciations of 'usury' were increasingly seen as irrelevant.) A Marxist *Merchant* is able to activate this contradiction, together with many low-toned ironies of the text, and play down the romantic, fairy-tale elements. Again, the early histories are fairly Brechtian. (And Brecht, be it added, was profoundly influenced by Shakespeare.) *King John* is a devastating analysis of kingship, and the director is entitled to emphasise the alienation of the leading character, in the Bastard's 'Mad world! mad kings! mad composition!' *Henry VI* is above all a disillusioned critique of the power process: and it contains, as Strehler points out, the only on-stage rebellion in the canon. What is always possible in the staging of these histories is that the audience should be made aware of the ongoing relevance of the action: and this, not through the crudities of contemporary costuming, but through subtler provocations. Giorgio Strehler seized on a passage of immense poignancy in *Henry VI, Part Three: Enter a son that has killed his father, dragging in the body . . . Enter a father that has killed his son, bringing in the body.* This is emblematic drama, drama which reduces the conflicting forces to two compelling images. Strehler, in giving full emphasis to this moment, made his actor wear a beast's mask — which he tore off in discovering the body's identity, to reveal an anguished human face. The audience is confronted with the human reality of the Civil Wars. Among the other possibilities, an emphasis upon a 'chorus' figure, a flowing sequence of scenes in the epic continuum, a calculated 'demystification' of kingship, all these are ways of animating the fundamental Shakespearian detachment and irony. Every director must come to terms with his own conception of history.

(iv)   *Abstract-eclectic*

And this may simply yield Peter Brook's position, which is that he is not interested in history. In that event, the main possibility seems this portmanteau category which I label, loosely, 'abstract-eclectic'. This is currently in the van of fashion. The setting, as bare as possible, conveys intimations of light and space. The Stratford 'white box' of 1972 is a leading instance. Brook's *Dream* setting suggested a gymnasium, a circus, a rehearsal room. While the setting remains open, the costumes may supply a diversity of stimuli. The theory, as stated by Peter Brook, is that consistency of costuming is the enemy; it is a superimposed schema, both stifling and distracting. He wishes to create via his costumes 'provocations' that identify themselves with no one era, national situation, or style. 'The necessity is that anything visual in a Shakespearian production should not confine the audience to a single attitude and a single interpretation.' This desire to keep the options open is very characteristic of today. A recent *Measure for Measure* was set against a background of bars and netting that could suggest either a prison or a football-ground barrier keeping back the spectators. The combination of freedom and diversity of allusion is what now appeals

to the directorial strategists. Trevor Nunn's black-leather Romans in a
raked white box could as well appear under this category as the
historical; Giorgio Strehler's *King Lear*, set in an empty plain that
could be a terrestrial planet or a cosmic circus points the same way.
By 'abstract' today one understands not the exoticisms of the Noguchi-
Gielgud *Lear*, but rather a setting implying the widest freedom in which
the director is able to generate his provocations.

These are the major strategies open to the director of today. In
pursuing one, he further defines his interpretation of the *current*
import of the text. It becomes the 'imaginative distortion', in Miller's
phrase, of the original myth. The production itself cannot be judged
on its supposed fidelity to the ur-text of the myth, the words of the
Folio. Rather, it must harness the myth's energies to a new pattern
that holds meaning for us. I cannot discover a formula for judgement
here. Certainly many productions are crude, eccentric, capricious,
insensitive. The myth has been 'de-natured'. But this is because most
enterprises in most fields fail to reach high standards. It does not
necessarily reflect a fundamental misconception of the challenge. Nor
will the metamorphosis of the director into the chairman of the actors'
board substantially modify the situation. And what, then, is the
situation? One comes back, perhaps, to Peter Brook's saying that one
needs a double attitude, of respect and disrespect – the dialectic is
what it's all about. Trevor Nunn accepts 'loyalty' rather than
'fidelity' to the text as the best guide. Or perhaps one comes ultimately
to the metaphors for Shakespeare that the directors choose. To
Jonathan Miller, Shakespeare today is part of an expanding universe,
dramatic matter continuously created out of fundamental substance
created centuries ago. To Peter Brook, Shakespeare is energy. The role
of Shakespeare is still to change the universal perception, and in
addressing themselves to his work the directors perceive it as life itself.

THE INTERVIEWS

JONATHAN MILLER

Ralph Berry Is there, today, anything in your letter to *The Times* that you would like to single out or modify?

Jonathan Miller No, I think that in a way that is the best brief expression of the point of view that I hold today. I think that I could amplify and enrichen some of the points but that really is, in a way, my basic manifesto about Shakespearian production. Can I say in a sense that my basic idea springs from one notion which comes not from the theatre, but from linguistic philosophy. It comes from a rather striking phrase of the Oxford philosopher, Peter Strawson, who in an essay when he was commenting on Bertrand Russell's theory of descriptions tried to account for the difficulties that Russell found himself in when trying to account for the meaning of certain sentences, which didn't refer to an actual historical personage but which nevertheless meant something, and were not nonsense. And Strawson emphasises that the reason why Russell got into this difficulty was that he forgot something very important about propositions. He said that it is not propositions which mean something but the people who mean things by the propositions which they utter. And I think that in the theatre what one has is a series of texts very many of which are almost bereft of collateral instructions telling one what the characters are and what they mean by what they say. All that you have are the utterances themselves. What you therefore have to do is to improvise and discover and embody people or personalities who might convincingly and consistently have meant something by all the utterances which happen to be written down opposite their name in the texts which we have inherited from the past.

RB It is clear then that you do not think of the Shakespeare text as having single, absolute, final meaning at all. You think of a multiplicity of meanings which it is the business of the director to project, or rather that it is the business of the director to select one and project that. But presumably you would not issue a licence to anybody on this. You would believe certain meanings as projected by directors could be, how shall we say, wrong, misleading, inadequate, not fully, not reasonably in accordance with the original text that has come down to us.

JM Yes. I think that there are extremes when one knows that the

29

text has been denatured beyond the point where anything satisfactory happens. It's not beyond the point of what the author intended — that, in a sense, is hardly what interests me. As I said in the letter, in a way the author's intentions are beyond guess. There is no way of finding out what he intended. Nevertheless there is a possibility of producing some sort of distortion or denaturing of the text. Now I can't produce any sort of recipe or a series of linguistic prescriptions in advance of any particular work which will allow one to say, 'This is what you mustn't do, ever!' Until an individual instance has been produced I wouldn't actually be able to say in advance how not to denature a text. I could say that certain given examples once they had occurred were instances of denatured text, but I couldn't tell in advance how not to do it.

RB Yes, I understand that. Could we move on to the question of how you personally go about the business of directing a Shakespeare play — what would you single out as the first step in the sequence?

JM Well, I think it varies from play to play. It varies from moment to moment in one's own career. I don't think there is, again, a set recipe or a series of ordered steps that one moves along in order to arrive at a full production. It happens in different ways, in different plays, as I say according to one's mood. Sometimes one has a very large, generalised notion about the overall meaning of the play, that may be a moral meaning, in terms of the individual human motives of the play which one has discerned in the text, or it may be some rather emblematic theme which one has extracted from the play as a whole, or it may be something much less generalised. One may almost in a sort of hallucinatory moment have overheard in one's mind's ear two phrases out of the play spoken and inflected in a certain way which then act as a sort of nucleus or a crystal which then consolidate the rest of the text, that if a given line is being spoken in a certain way or a certain tone of voice, with a certain form or a certain inflexion, then other inflexions must follow from it in other parts of the text which one has not overheard in this way, and very often a production will start from one hallucinatory inflexion which one has overheard in one's mind's ear when thinking about, or perhaps when not even thinking about it; it may just suddenly come out of the blue.

RB This inflexion then is not something which in the first instance occurs from an actor, this is something that occurs to you personally in your mind alone.

JM Often before I've ever met any actors and before I've actually seen a cast who might be used to inflect it in that way. It is like one of

those spirit voices that suddenly speaks in the street and you hear it
uttering a line in a certain way and the way in which that line is
uttered bends the rest of the play accordingly. I can give you an example. When I was going to do *The Merchant of Venice* — I was
asked to do *The Merchant of Venice*, so that in a sense the initiative
for doing the play in the first place was not mine, therefore I didn't
approach the play with some generalised notion to begin with. But
having been asked to do it the play entered my imagination at a
subconscious level and without any prompting or intention or
deliberation on my part. On one evening I wasn't doing anything in
particular, but I overheard in my mind's ear Portia speaking the line
'the quality of mercy is not strained' and in place of the ringing
feminine rhetoric of the familiar version, I heard and saw a brief flash
in which I saw a rather boyish figure leaning forward over a table on
one elbow saying those first lines in a rather irritable, explanatory tone
of voice, as if trying to push something which someone rather
stupidly misunderstood previously saying (well, I can't reproduce it
accurately), 'the quality of mercy is not *strained*' and in that tone
with the weight placed on strained and the visual weight placed on
elbow on a table, certain consequences came from that. First of all,
the visual image of the table meant that I could no longer place that
thing in a courtroom. People do not sit and lean across tables in
courtrooms, they can only sit and lean across tables in small chambers,
like Justices' chambers, off the main courtroom. Once I had seen
that, that meant that there were only certain settings which could
accommodate that hallucination and this became a nineteenth-century
setting in which someone could quite realistically plead a cause in a
judge's room and out of that suddenly the production began to take
its form, from that tiny unrepresentative nucleus.

   RB So a production with you has a moment of conception, and
thereafter the idea having formed, this idea is allowed to form, to
dominate the multitude of other considerations.

   JM Yes.

   RB Which you must then organise.

   JM Yes, that's right and then, in a sense, the image of it is rather
like a candelabrum, this central thing becomes the thing from which
the whole thing is hung, and then there are a whole series of dependent
ornaments which fall from that central conception. Although, in fact,
as far as the play is concerned it may not be a central conception. it's
only central in that that was the one that initiated the first step. As the
play then develops other interests may shift the emphasis, but the

emphasis would not shift in the way that they had shifted had it not started in that particular hallucination.

RB What seems fascinating to me here, is that your approach has, from the outset, destroyed the cliché. The cliché is that the speech is a set piece, which has no context, it being the set piece. You have however envisaged the speech within a context, and this at once over-leaps the barriers between the original event and the production, that had been formed over the centuries.

JM Well, in a sense I am lucky in that I am ignorant of the theatre. I have never been a theatre enthusiast; in the past I didn't go very much to the theatre, and therefore I had no knowledge really of the standard ways of doing a play. Therefore lines come to me and inflexions, notions and ideas about the plays come to me without that decoration and corrosion of previous ideas. Now some people may look upon this as a drawback. They say, 'Oh well, you're actually an amateur in the theatre,' but I think, in fact, it is this amateur status which allows one to see the thing for the first time, and in that way it is not so much fighting against a cliché, because I don't know the clichés very well. It is just simply that I haven't been exposed to them, and therefore have not been seduced by them.

RB I see the great value of this. Could I ask you to elaborate one point that you made? You spoke of the table being a necessity of the production because of the original concept, and that the concept became identified with the nineteenth century. Could you elaborate on the fitness of the nineteenth century for your production of *The Merchant of Venice*?

JM Well, of course, having committed myself to a nineteenth-century framework as a result of a purely accidental exposure to an image, I then had to examine the congruence of that setting with the rest of the text and the more I examined it, the more it actually seemed more than congruent, but actually very illuminating. The nineteenth-century setting brought out and emphasised interesting features of the status of the intelligent woman, the woman stultified by the domination of men, the domination of fathers and suitors. A woman with enough intelligence to plead with great eloquence and success and wit and guile in a courtroom, suddenly starts to vibrate with an interesting intensity in the nineteenth-century setting. Similarly the theme, albeit subdued and subtle, of the homosexual relationship between Bassanio and Antonio, has a subtle and rich over-tone without necessarily being explicit in the relationship between Oscar Wilde and Lord Alfred Douglas. I didn't wish to see this as a

roman-à-clef, and I didn't wish to illustrate the dilemma of Oscar
Wilde and the homosexuality of Oscar Wilde, but very often in works
of art they achieve their richness and their appeal because of the
overtones which you strike when you use a certain image. Audiences
who were, as it were, familiar with the tradition and the culture at
large, could scarcely avoid at least thinking, or bringing that colour
of knowledge to the image that you supply, not because you wish to
say specifically that this is Oscar Wilde and Lord Alfred Douglas, but
that by being aware of the fact that it is similar to the situation of
Wilde and Bosey the dilemma is somehow re-enforced by being seen
to be part of the general problem.

RB The historical context certainly makes a difference there. It's
obviously true that, for instance, an eighteenth-century setting would
achieve nothing for the particular points you had in mind.

JM No, I mean, I think that there are other slants, other ways of
cutting the crystal which would bring out different sorts of appearance
and illumination which the eighteenth century would do. I don't quite
know what they are at the moment, but I can imagine something of
interest in that setting. I can imagine something of interest in almost
every setting that one chooses. I would say that one of the ways in
which the greatness of Shakespeare shows itself is by the multiplicity
of the setting in which he can be played with profit and value.

RB One of the advantages of Shakespeare is that some three and a
half centuries and a lot of history have elapsed since his death. The
director, therefore, has an ever-widening pool of history to allude to.

JM Yes. You see I mean, I think that one of the nice things about
art is that history somehow presents itself to you as a simultaneous
volume of events in which all events are happening at the same time,
all equally accessible, all mutually referable and each individual item
enriched and complicated by the fact that it somehow implies every
other event to which it is similar in that volume of history in which it
takes place.

RB At the same time, however, history has to happen in order, and
some material must wait for its time. There seems to be an excellent
example of this with your production of *The Tempest*. I take it that we
have had to wait until the twentieth century to receive many of the
possibilities in *The Tempest*.

JM Yes, I think that some of the notions of colonialism, and I am
not thinking of the crude, radical view of the immorality of colonialism,
but some of the ways in which we visualise the ironies of colonialism
have only become available to us since we have seen the break-up of the

colonial system and of the colonial mind. This in a sense is a general point, it happens in disease, we can often only understand natural processes in dissolution, because in dissolution we begin to see the component parts and how they are related to one another. It's in disease that one understands health and I think that we can actually now by hindsight understand a great deal more of the relationship of white Europe to the black world. Knowing what we now know about the emergence of the black world and its revolt against the world of white Europe, I just don't think that we would have had the conceptual apparatus, the cognitive skills to visualise that until it began to break down. Now this is not because I wish to seize *The Tempest* or to hijack *The Tempest* and to fly it to a modern airport and make it do the work of anti-colonial radicalism, that would be I think a very crude and brutal thing to do. It is just that by bringing out that particular theme in *The Tempest* something rather rich happens which wouldn't occur if one simply played the rather romantic version of *The Tempest* where both Caliban and Ariel are impalpable spirits or gross clods. I mean I think that there is something very interesting also in seeing the trio of Prospero, Caliban and Ariel in the light of some metaphysical idea of the division of the human soul and the tripartite nature of the mind.

RB How did your approach to *The Tempest* come into being?

JM Well, it came into being in two ways. Very often I find that, although I spoke previously about not being exposed to theatrical clichés I've been exposed to a certain number of them and certainly some of my moves in the theatre have been prompted by a revulsion against certain well-established clichés, which are so glaring that hardly anyone who is aware of simply being at school could fail to notice them. Now the one which stuck in my gorge was the sequin-spangled, pointed-eared, flitting figure of Ariel on wires, his hands held stiffly behind him as a flew *à la* Peter Pan on and off the stage. This seemed to me to be sentimental and diminishing and similarly the scaly, web-footed monster of Caliban just didn't tell me anything about anyone, it wasn't a monster which meant anything in my imagination and it actually clotted my imagination and stopped it from thinking. But I had been reading some years before a book by an anthropologist called Mannoni, who had written a book on the revolt in Madagascar in 1947, and he had used as a metaphor in order to explain the relationships of the very protagonists of the revolt the image of *The Tempest* and he saw Caliban and Ariel as different forms of black response to white paternalism. In Caliban he saw the demoralised, detribalised, dispossessed shuffling field hand and in Ariel a rather deft accomplished black who actually absorbs all the techniques and skills of the white master; the house servant, who is then in a position to assume political power when the white master goes back home. And of course we had this situation only a few years ago in Nigeria, with the skilled civil servant Ibos and the unskilled tribal Hausas. Now once again I wasn't using *The Tempest* as a political cartoon to illustrate the Nigerian dilemma nor as it were to castigate modern colonialism or to expose the wickedness of Rhodesia, but to use the images of Rhodesia, Nigeria, and indeed the whole colonial theme as knowledge which the audience brought to bear on Shakespeare's play. They could scarcely avoid thinking of that situation when the two characters were represented as blacks. Now by doing it in this way I hoped to bring them into a closer relationship with the whole notion of subordination and mastery which I think is one of the things which Shakespeare is talking about with great eloquence in that play. And I think he is also talking about, in a sense, infantilism and about the way in which maturity is only arrived at by surrendering one's claim to control the whole of nature. A child after all arrives at maturity by appreciating the reality principle, and after all what is the reality principle? The reality principle is simply the understanding that there are certain things over which one has control, and there are most things over which one has no control.

RB I think that the reality principle is certainly one of the immutable touchstones of Shakespeare's whole work.

JM I think that this in a sense comes out very clearly in this play, particularly if you slant it in this manner. After all one of the most important aspects of the reality principle is that there is a limited control over other people's destinies, not just over the physical world, but over the moral world, and that certain infantile personalities flourish in the colonial situation because they meet people whose power to resist their will is diminished by their lack of skills and so you often get rather immature personalities flourishing in the colonial situation because the colonial situation has in it people who cannot resist the superior technology of advanced society, and Prospero achieves his maturity in surrendering his power over his slaves, in leaving the island and returning to the world in which he must actually face his peers and equals, in a society where everyone has access to the same skills.

RB And indeed he looks forward to surrendering his power to his children.

JM He surrenders three things: he surrenders the power over his own children, he surrenders the power over subordinates, or at least over helpless subordinates, and he surrenders this impractical desire for power over the forces of nature. By breaking his staff he is doing what the child really does after the age of five, of realising that his rage will not call down the tempest but only contempt.

RB You've spoken eloquently of your concept of *The Tempest* as of *The Merchant of Venice*. How do you now go about the business of translating your concept with all its ramifications into stage language that the audience will be able to pick up?

JM That's a very difficult question because again there is no prescription and no recipe, there is no advanced instruction that one can refer to. In the first place you simply elicit from the actors those inflexions and tones which illustrate those moral ideas which interest you at the time. You do this by simply explaining to the actor what you feel the leading salient issues of the play are for you at that moment, making it quite clear to them that you do not regard this as the definitive, final interpretation. This is simply a provisional hypothesis which must eventually be superseded, but nevertheless convincing them that for the moment it stands as a convincing hypothesis and they can illustrate it by standing in certain ways, bending their voices in certain ways and adopting ways of speech which they had not previously used. In addition to that you frame the production with all sorts of visual accessories which emphasise your point. Sometimes they may be elaborate emblems which you hope the audience will interpret correctly; even if they don't interpret in detail or explicitly you hope that it will set up suggestive overtones in their imaginations which will assist their understanding in the direction which you feel is important. What I try to do is to create as much complexity and indeed as it were strategic ambiguity as I can in the production. Ambiguity in Empson's sense, that I choose a cluster of meanings which are centred around the salient issue, but which nevertheless are not just simply that issue alone. I think if you choose clear-cut explicit lines what you get is fairly boring, instructive theatre whereas if you create clusters of meanings, so long as those clusters are centred around a salient point, then I think you get theatrical art, as indeed I think you get poetic art in this way, you create very carefully centred, rich clusters of related ambiguous overtones.

RB Do the actors cause you significantly to modify your view of the play during rehearsal, or do they rather, as it were, add to your concept?

JM I think they almost always add to the concept. I can't think of any production in which I've departed from whatever it was that set me going on the play with enthusiasm in the first place. I don't regard the additions as accessory ornaments either; they are integral, in so far as if I accept them and incorporate them then they are actually part of the bone and muscle of the production, and they are often bones and muscles which I have not conceived or anticipated before I've started, and the great mystery and excitement of rehearsing and direct-ing a play is the discovery of themes and items and features which are congruent with one's first intention, consistent with it, but nevertheless not anticipated at the time when you actually had that intention. Now you may ask how that happens. I think that what happens is that the first step perhaps in successful directing or rehearsing is the telling of an eloquent story at the start of the rehearsal which creates a frame of mind, a tilt to the collective imagination of all those involved which makes it inevitable that whatever invention is thrown up within that group will be bound to enrich and enlarge the comparatively spare and simple idea that you had up till now.

RB This telling of an eloquent story: does this mean that you personally will address the company at length about the play and the meanings that you have perceived?

JM Yes. I mean I will often start with a prepared speech, or rela-tively prepared, which I will then improvise as I go along on the first day. I tend to rehearse in a very haphazard and indolent way. I have never set programmes, I don't block very clearly as I go along. I think my rehearsals are marked more by talk and tea-breaks than by what one would call hard, regimented work and the actual moments of rehearsal in a sense are glosses upon the conversations which are running throughout the period of rehearsal, rather than the other way around. They are not as it were breaks from the hard work, the hard work is a consequence of the conversations which we have had.

RB How for instance do you deal with a technical point on this level, when an actor asks you for guidance on some point such as: Claudius says, 'Have you heard the argument? Is there no offence in it?' To whom does Claudius speak this line, and with what inflexion?

JM Well, sometimes one has it very clearly in mind before one starts, you know, because of the framework that you have established to begin with, and that is already, as it were, pre-planned long before the actor comes to the text; that is not very often. In the case of *The Merchant of Venice*, it was as I described it, already set up before I began, it was the occasion for doing the whole production. But in very many cases we discover in the process of rehearsal, to whom he must have said it because in a sense what we do jointly is to conjure up the person who meant something by that line and once conjured up he can only speak it in a certain way to a certain person. I often think of the process of rehearsal as being very similar to a spiritualist séance. The warmth and social incandescence created by the certain kinds of rehearsals, by the conviviality which you establish as a director, favour the arrival of voices which will seem to have meant something by the lines which they then utter. I think of these characters in Shakespeare's plays, or indeed in anyone's plays, as absconded personalities who are not yet there, who have a script prepared in advance for them, of which we do not know the precise meaning until they are conjured out of the air and actually speak through the lines.

RB Are they absconded personalities in the sense that everybody is an absconded personality?

JM Not strictly. I mean that I think that in a sense everyone is an absconded personality, that we do not know who any of us really are, but in this particular case we are deprived of even the slender possibility that we have in ordinary social life of getting to know them. We will never be, and no one ever has been, introduced to Hamlet. I think of Hamlet as a series of lines to which an infinite series of claimants arrives and competes for. I sometimes think of the Tichborne claimant. Hamlet is someone who might be someone, were there to be someone to claim him, and I think the job of rehearsal is to create a circumstance in which claimants will present themselves for examination.

RB Now we come to a slightly delicate area. To follow up your metaphor, it is quite clear that some claimants can establish an overwhelming case if they can arrange for certain parts of the evidence to be tactfully laid aside for the duration. I have known for instance, Hamlets too delicate to enunciate the line, 'I'll lug the guts into the neighbour room.' What happens when you find certain portions of the text that are not as fully congruent as you would wish with the main lines of your interpretation?

JM I will sometimes cut them. I don't feel any real guilt about this. The text is always there to be claimed by the next competitor who might be able to fit the role without such surgery, and I have cut things. I have often cut rather famous lines. On the whole I try to re-inflect the lines in such a way that they can be retained and still be congruent with the features of the claimant that I am backing at that moment.

RB In a sense, of course, cutting is a direct and honest procedure. The alternative so often is to retain the line, but neutralise it or throw it away.

JM I think that actually there is no such thing as throwing away a line. I think that almost all lines that are supposedly thrown away are simply inflected in a way that they lose apparent importance or become unnoticeable. Nevertheless there is an active decision about how they are going to be inflected — so long as they are retained they are dealt with in one way or another. Often it becomes a very complicated problem this, and you will often spend hours over one of these indigestible features of the text, which means fighting with the features of the claimant that you are backing.

RB In any event we know that surely Shakespeare's plays must have been cut consistently throughout the contemporary performances, as they are today.

JM I think that there are no rules or regulations about this at all. Each generation tends to regard certain lines as the crucial ones, but that is because that generation has decided to focus upon one particular plane of interest or meaning within the play, and within that plane certain lines obviously assume a dazzling precedence. Another generation will focus on another plane within which a different set of lines will assume a precedence. Merely because certain lines have become very very famous, so famous as to be almost part of the fundamental tool kit of little cartoonists, doesn't mean that one is therefore obliged to choose the plane of meaning within which those lines have always had their precedence. I'm always moved by one particular story in connection with this. When the paintings of Vermeer were first forged by Van Meegeren in the late thirties, early forties, the artefacts that were produced were so convincing, so faithful that they took in very large numbers of art experts. Thirty years later the same pictures were presented to art experts of some standing, admittedly in the knowledge that they were forgeries; and these art experts were puzzled as to how anyone was ever taken in by the forgery. Not only do they know that they're forgeries, but they cannot understand how anyone was ever deluded into thinking they were anything but forgeries. Now this is not simply because in the intervening thirty years connoisseurship has improved, certainly not by that amount, but as Gombrich points out, it is due to the fact that anyone wishing to forge Vermeer in 1940 has chosen to do so because he has seen in Vermeer values and interests upon which he will focus and which he will emphasise when producing his forgery. Someone looking at Vermeer in 1970 is forging a different object because he has decided upon certain values which for him are interesting so that even when the

purpose of the game is fidelity, fidelity indeed to the point of decep-
tion, departure from the original is unavoidable. And in exactly the
same way, in producing a play, exactly the same thing operates. Each
period focuses on a play and projects into it interests and pre-
occupations and prejudices of that time in such a way that even if
it's trying to be faithful it will produce a different object to someone
working thirty years later, with the same commitment to fidelity,
but who is nevertheless forced away from the original version by his
particular interests. Now if this can happen with a work of visual art,
when after all you are going from one object of the visual order to
another object of the visual order, think how much larger the opportunities for departure are when in a play you're going from an object
of printed order to an object of the performed order.

   RB Yes, indeed. What then do you understand, if anything is to
be understood, by fidelity to Shakespeare's texts?

   JM I really hardly think of the term at all. I think that fidelity is
the job of forgers and of map-makers and of engineers/draughtsmen.
The job of the artist in the theatre is illumination and reconstruction
and the endless task of assimilating the objects of the past into the
interests of the present, on the understanding that the physical artefact
which is the occasion for such an enterprise will be retained in some
place in its original form, so that it is available for anyone else who
wishes to make a competitive reconstruction of his own. It's an
expanding universe, there is no end to it, it is a continuous creation,
rather as the cosmologists have shown us the universe is. I think that
it may well be that in a thousand years' time we will scarcely recognise
the reconstructions which have been wreaked upon Shakespeare, and I
don't think therefore that a thousand years later the vandalism will
have grown larger, all that will have happened is that the universe has
expanded and that literary and dramatic matter is being continuously
created out of fundamental substance created in the early history of
the literary universe.

KONRAD SWINARSKI

Ralph Berry I'd like to ask you first, and very generally, why you choose to direct Shakespeare.

Konrad Swinarski I think it was a coincidence in the beginning. I was asked to do a Shakespeare play in West Germany, and I did *Twelfth Night*, and then I got more and more interested in Shakespeare. The productions I've done here, in Poland, were *All's Well That Ends Well* and *A Midsummer Night's Dream*. I did them for many reasons. It was the third time I'd done *All's Well*: I'd done it once in West Germany and it was not really understood. I did it a second time in Scandinavia, in Finland, and I considered that it was still not understood. I went on working on it, and did it for the third time in Poland; and then, suddenly, it was somehow understood. So my version of this play, or my vision of this play, belongs to this country and this people. I've discussed it with the actors here, and I could see the reactions of the audience. I've discovered that Shakespearian interpretation consists not only of reading Shakespeare, but means a kind of society that understands you and can accept this kind of interpretation, let's say a black interpretation of a Shakespeare comedy . . . Why did I choose this play? Because *All's Well* has its own tradition in our history of the theatre, and it was interpreted as a kind of fairy tale for years and has never been done since the war. It was my private interest to discover the play once more from the beginning, in all its depth and double meanings, and to produce it for an audience that could pick up all the double meanings of this kind of so-called black comedy.

RB If I understand you correctly, then, you are saying that it is not so much a matter of Shakespeare as a general playwright that interests you, it is rather the fact of certain plays by Shakespeare that seem to you at a given time strikingly relevant to the society that you have in mind.

KS No, that's not true, because what you do and how you do it depend on the immediate situation. Of course many other Shakespeare plays could be done here at the same time, but I just picked up *All's Well* and *A Midsummer Night's Dream* because I could cast the plays the way I wanted them. I just don't have the actors to do Shakespeare's tragedies here, otherwise I would have done them. I think that I could do other Shakespearian productions in Warsaw, where there are so many theatres, but you never find an entirely satisfactory cast in one theatre; you have the Hamlet in one theatre and then you have another 22 theatres to find the King.

RB Could you tell me more about *All's Well*, and the reasons, apart naturally from the accidents of casting, that induced you to put it on?

KS Look, I think that life is not very funny, but I like to play with it, and I picked on this kind of comedy because I think it is a picture of a world that is very similar to the world I'm living in and collaborating with; and I'm trying to show its face.

RB How did you go about the business of preparing *All's Well* for the stage?

KS I think I read this play first in a very simple way, I mean comparing it with our conditions. Maybe it's not so simple, but it's a useful way of discovering all the human relationships in the play. Of course, for us a Court is a Court; in spite of being a socialistic country we have a feudal society, which means that the Court in our country is a kind of power which finally determines what is going on between people. And then I read in a Polish review from the early twentieth or late nineteenth century that it's a very dirty play that should never have been printed; the translator said that he respects Shakespeare so much that he has translated this kind of dirty play only because of his respect for Shakespeare, not for the moral sense of the play. I think it's an edition of 1897 (in Poland), and it fascinated me, what the translator called moral and what he called immoral in the play. And then I went on picking up all the 'immoral' things in that play. For that translator, no one was a positive person, there is no happy ending, and he discovered Shakespeare's plan with the title *All's Well That Ends Well. Nothing* ends well in this play, but he was not going to elaborate this idea, he simply gave this message to the audience, which one could read or not. The translator does it for Shakespeare, but he doesn't want to destroy people's vision of that wonderful poet. And that was somehow the next point I started with. Now, all the human relationships: the first thing I discovered is that the whole story between Bertram and Parolles is really a homosexual story, which is based on the intrigue of Lafeu to get Parolles for himself, to deliver Bertram from Parolles, and to be useful to the King in this way while suiting his own interests. And in this play, you have scenes where you discover all the relationships. In the first rehearsal, I suddenly discovered that the final scene works perfectly if you have a kind of tableau on stage, who is with whom, who is against whom, so that the only possible solution is for Parolles to be together with Lafeu for him to speak the last lines about the handkerchief, and 'Wait on me home, I'll make sport with thee.' Diana is together with her mother, Helena is with Bertram, and in between are the King and the Countess who are managing the whole business concerning the two young people, having their own interests to pursue. It was not easy to judge from the beginning if the whole set of relationships could be brought into a final scene on stage, but suddenly I realised that there must have been a rule governing the way people were placed on stage — where they were standing, what they were telling, in order to indicate that their relationship has been, let's say, arranged in the right way.

RB How then did you depict theatrically the final positions in the relationships — to take the main point first, how do you see the future as between Bertram and Helena?

KS I think it's obvious — she's pregnant by him, but she's not finding the happiness she was looking for. She has discovered that the desire to have him, to conquer him, is futile because in the end he will not be her husband really, merely a figure. Even though she's pregnant by him, she realises that he is not the main point, and that what she has won is a part of a human career, but not a part of a human being.

RB And how did you project this on stage?

KS It is through the last entrance, when she enters the Court, and she sees how Bertram is lying to the King in order to remain in good standing with him, which means that he cares much more for his future career than he cares for human feelings. At this moment she gives up, because she sees it has nothing to do with human feelings, it has all been a game in order to go on making a career in the Court before the King.

RB So the actress displays quite clearly her feelings that she has lost, essentially.

KS I tried to help her, because when she appears on stage being pregnant, let's say eight months gone, the Countess comes close to her, and she immediately picks up her belly. It is a young human being discovering the world that older people prepare for something other than the fulfilment of young lives and young love. The older generation is fulfilling *its* life through renewing the family, via the son.

RB This is of course an exceptionally difficult play. From what you have said it seems that your Bertram is a rather unattractive young man, and you do not try to conceal this.

KS No, he's not unattractive, but he is a young man who in the beginning is somehow faithful to his friend Parolles, but point by point he is broken by society, which means in his case by Lafeu, who wants to draw him away from his friend and make him want to be a good servant to the King. He wants to bring Bertram to a normal life — that is, to marry, have children, and be a normal son of a feudal family.

RB This is a play, too, in which it is vital to assess the direction of the energies, if you like, which are generated by the peripheral figures. I am thinking particularly of the King, the Countess, the Clown, Lafeu, and Parolles. How do you see these figures?

KS So let's start with the King. I think he's somebody who's not very old, but he's old through his knowledge of the world. He knows that everything in this world can be managed in politics. He knows a great deal about war, and knows immediately how to handle the war as such. He lets the young people go but he does not let the government participate in the war. He knows that the young people need the war as a kind of experience, but on the other hand he knows that the government doesn't have to participate officially. He knows all the feudal moves: when he writes a letter to the Duke of Florence, and sends it through the French lords, it's a very diplomatic letter, saying I'm not going to oppose you or abandon you, but I'm supporting you only with young people, not with the state power. The young people are very willing to fight, because they are young enough not to know what they are doing; all they care about is the next year at Court, and they can make their career only through fighting. It is their only opportunity. Or look at the brothers Dumain, who collaborate with the Court as in effect official spies — in the diplomatic service.

But back to the King: I think that he understands the world, and that he doesn't want to direct the government, he wants much more to direct life. And then Helena comes, who belongs to a different kind of society, and is a kind of bourgeois daughter. The physician, her father, the only one he believed in, is somebody he remembers with gratitude. And there are two reasons for him to help Helena. First of all, he does not believe in the distinctions between classes, and the whole story about blood in the original sources is a story of human relationships out of class. And he respects new life as being something vital, as bringing society further on to a new stage. He treats Bertram as being the son of his friend. There is nothing told explicitly about the connection between Bertram's father and the King, but anyhow it must have been a very deep human connection, for he wants to make out of Bertram someone who could prolong the memory of his connection with his father, whatever it was. He looks on Bertram as someone who needs to grow up but has sufficient life-force to prolong the family. I think he knows everything about the relationship between

Parolles and Bertram: there are no straight lines about that, but when you make it clear on the stage it is apparent enough. The one who helps him is Lafeu. Lafeu is a kind of Minister of Interior Affairs, and maybe more, because they have something in common. When Lafeu enters the scene (II, 1) they talk about, let's say mental and sexual relationships, and Lafeu tries to introduce Helena to the King. When he mentions the story of Pandarus ('I am Cressid's uncle,/That dare leave two together') — I think that they understand one another very well. Now the King gives Helena her chance, and he wants to find out what is going to happen. Of course it has to be arranged on the stage in a particular way, and I have edited the scene showing how Helena cures the King; she does a kind of massage.

RB Did you depict the massage as having specifically sexual overtones?

KS No, like every massage it was half sexual! It was only half, but anyhow the King suddenly discovers that he can move, and Helena brings him to the point when he gets up — she helps him to stand up. It continues like this: she starts to walk with him, then all of a sudden she starts dancing with him, counting the steps one, two, three, four, one, two, three, four, then it turns into a kind of Court dance with the whole cast. Naturally I supported it with music, the musicians who belong to the Court suddenly arrive on stage and are terribly surprised when the King gets up, and they start to play. It's a big surprise for the rest of the Court (as well as for Lafeu and Bertram), they immediately appear and see the King moving. But that is not the end of the King's story. In the fifth Act, when he sees what he has accomplished as the new director of life, trying to find happiness for Bertram and for Helena, he discovers that his direction is completely false, that Bertram cares only for his career, while Helena discovers that she is only a point in a game which does not bring young people together in love. She has been used. And he goes on playing this comedy, but he knows that he has not created happiness, he has created merely a new misunderstanding in human relationships. In his Epilogue, he asks for applause — maybe you can help, when he turns to the audience — so he is deeply in doubt whether a human being can rule the country, and can rule life. He asks the audience through their applause to help the life that is directed by a human being. And at the end it must be played in such a way that he visibly doubts this possibility of a human being creating and ruling his own life.

RB It seems to me that the King must have been the central figure in your production, and that the King expresses the final position that you wish the entire production to take.

KS Not exactly, I wouldn't say that: the King is very important, but I think that the truth lies between the characters, because Lafeu looking at the King could still express his opinion, and the Countess could express her opinion of the King's wishes in the same way. The King has the Epilogue, and must therefore be the last person to speak. But we went on with a whole final scene where we played the King's desire to bring the people together, and he's giving up the hope of Diana and her mother to make a career in the Court, the bitter situation of Parolles coming together with Lafeu and Lafeu, shall we say, being the winner of the whole story. And the bitter situation of Helena and Bertram — they know everything about themselves and about each other, but they go on playing the game in order to serve the King. It was done in a kind of pantomime, they were all dancing together so it could be shown; and in the end the fool Lavache is left smiling over the whole situation, which through his experience he has known in advance and almost from the beginning of the play.

RB Lavache, then, is above all the man who knows.

KS Yes: he's very old, but he still doesn't know everything. I wouldn't say he knows from the beginning of the play what's going to happen. He knows every human relationship, between the younger people as well as the older ones. And of course he's danced with the Countess, and he plays a game with her. She goes on playing a game with Lavache to satisfy herself — she is of an age where to be desired is much more than to be bedded. Lavache has a real human feeling for the Countess, and would like to have a relationship with her, but he plays the game that he is allowed to play. He cannot come too close, because in the feudal sense he is not a friend of hers, he serves her.

RB He's a surrogate courtier.

KS Yes, but in the feudal situation he cannot come too close. And of course you can play this game out (possible at that time), so that he even puts his hand under her skirt, whereupon she tells the offender he is going too far, because she would have to give up her position as Countess compared to a man from the lowest social stratum. But he knows the world, and is experienced enough to go on playing that game. He knows that human life is based mostly on sexual relations, something which he expresses through many things in the play, and he is telling it to the Countess; she knows it but cannot accept it. He knows about the relationship between Bertram and Helena, and about the relationship between Bertram and Parolles, and exactly what Lafeu wants; and he knows about the letters the

Countess writes, but his basic sentence is about the unfulfilled sexual relations between human beings. That's why he is wise; that's what he cracks jokes about and everybody understands it has a double meaning. He really understands most of the human relations in the play.

RB So, in a play that seems to be concerned primarily with social values, the Clown is the most explicit representative of the idea that what matters most in human affairs is sex.

KS Yes: he knows it, and he knows also what can cover sex and cause people to fight with each other, fight with themselves, to try to maintain their social position, or ladder, or career. He knows that sex can be the motor, the first movement, but he knows also the relativity of straight sex in life. He knows all the circumstances, he knows what real love is and what corrupted love is.

RB What, overall, is your view of *All's Well*?

KS Look, I think when I compare this play with life here in my country, it's a kind of story, it might even sound a fantastic story which has a lot of black . . .

RB Humour?

KS Not only black humour, it has a lot of humour but it has finally undefined black definition. Its statement is that human nature cannot b be ruled by human nature, that happiness in life cannot be solved by a good King, that war is a kind of human experience which can be very cruel; but finally all the people agree to go on lying about the world that they live in, making a compromise, making a horrible compromise, in order for life to go on in spite of being dirty, in spite of being undefined, and that is something that compared to the conditions I have lived in is a kind of realistic theatre.

RB And indeed, in the conditions that we have all lived in, I think, realistic theatre. You've concentrated upon certain very dynamic areas in the text, especially the areas of social hierarchy and government power, of sex, and of the necessary compromises that society must make in order to function at all. And this approach to *All's Well* highlights the quality of the play that we rather crudely draw attention to, normally, by calling it a 'problem play' — in company, invariably, with *Troilus and Cressida, Measure for Measure*, and sometimes with other plays of this period of Shakespeare's work. Can I ask you now to tell me something of your *Midsummer Night's Dream*, which I think you take as touching the areas of concern associated with the problem plays, but rather earlier (1595 or so) than we normally think of as the beginning of the problem plays.

KS Maybe for one reason, that I did *All's Well* first and *A Mid-*

summer Night's Dream later, I took a lot of the first experience into the second play. It was funny but bitter as well. Now what does the play mean to us today? First of all I've told you already that in spite of being a socialistic country we are still a kind of feudal society, because there is still a ladder with somebody who is down, and somebody who is up. And of course a Court in Poland is immediately identified with some kind of governmental business, and I did follow that line in a way because I turned the costumes into Court from the Polish Baroque period. So they were Polish nobles dealing with Polish problems, because the problems of Egeus and Hermia and Helena and the young men are for us a conflict between the young and old generations, and the Court (of Theseus, in this case) has to solve the problem and has to decide whom it is for. For a long time he tries to get out of this difficulty, and Nature finally decides for Theseus what he has to be for. The young people in the end find themselves the way they would wish. But behind this is the story of Titania and Oberon, which has to be interpreted in my country in a certain way. Of course they are gods. What do gods mean to us? They are free. They live more than one human life, and they have much more experience than one single life here can. All the mythological background is used to depict a couple staying together but having different interests in the world. Titania is now taking over the power in this, let's say fantastic government, having the fairies; Oberon has his fairies too, but they have already divided their kingdom into two parts, so that Oberon has the final decision in what he wants to do, but he cares much more for sensual life, and the Queen, Titania, cares much more for harmony in the kingdom.

RB 'Harmony' you take to include the commitment to past relationships, which is the reason Titania gives for not handing over the changeling that Oberon desires?

KS Yes, I'd say Titania wants more and more control in ruling the country, and she cuts down every human sensual relationship — that's the reason why Oberon tries to punish her with Bottom. Now having these two lovers here is not only a fantastic story, it is a sexual story and a political story in one. But I think the most important thing is of a kind that there hasn't even been in this country — there are still Courts that are above us which might have a different kind of independence, a different order of human behaviour: they are not bound to any other Court any more. But in *A Midsummer Night's Dream* you have many levels, you have Titania and Oberon, you have the Court which is already bound to a situation, and you have a

third level, the craftsmen and working classes. To me, the main point
became this: I could not understand why in *A Midsummer Night's
Dream* the fifth Act is just an epilogue. Everything is finished, they are
in full harmony, having found each other, and the Duke's very happy
because everything has gone the way he wanted it. And then you have
the third group, the workers, who provide an Epilogue by putting on a
show, but I still believe that Shakespeare intended to hold a mirror
to the Court through the workers. Of course it is easy to identify
symbols here, and we tried to show the Moon as a kind of allegory of
human desires and human dreams, to show the Lion as a kind of
governmental power, and the Wall as being the older generation
separating the young lovers. The moment you establish all the symbols
like that, you can go on to relate who does understand the real story,
because on the one side Theseus understands everything, he understands the correspondences, and who else could there be? I think
Hippolyta understands them (but she doesn't respect them), and the
man who wrote the play, Quince.

There was an actors' group with the man who wrote the play,
consisting of Bottom, the man who plays Thisbe, and two or three
more. They're not professional actors, they're amateurs, and they are
delegated from the unions, which is natural enough here but which is
also in Shakespeare's lines. They meet for the first time, and he looks
at them and invents his play, scene by scene, for the first version of
the play is different from the last one which he puts on in front of the
Court. He uses one for the powerful Lion, and one for the Moon —
there must be something in their expression to cast them like that,
and uses one for the Wall. They are not professionals, but they know
that something can be accomplished in front of the Court, but they are
frightened of going too far in case they are punished for it. The old man
who writes the play, Quince, is completely aware of everything, and he
is not frightened to put his vision of the world to the test in front of
the Court. It might sound very complicated, but I think it *is* very
complicated, and very true to life. Now the man who plays the Lion,
Snug, and the one who plays the Moon, and the third one who is the
Wall, they don't know what they are playing. Quince uses them, and is
glad they don't understand the meaning. He produces a play that is
deeply linked with the story of the Court during the recent period, and
you have the line and acting when Theseus comes and says, 'you are
very well' because the line was punishing someone and they are brought
by the Moon because human fantasy is not very useful in the Court.
The young people follow Theseus' lead, and are already completely

corrupted by the Court. They only try to support Theseus in what they think is his opinion. But Theseus is wiser than the young people, and he permits the play to be produced, even though it speaks the truth about the life of the Court. And he allows it to go on to the end, but when it comes to the Epilogue, he says, 'No epilogue, I pray you ... But come, your Bergomask,' which to us is a kind of folk dance. Of course we dance folk dances everywhere when we don't speak the truth about the government. So it has a double meaning in my country: the folk dance is a substitute for the truth being told. The truth would be the Epilogue he never speaks. And I think it is the story of the man who wrote the play, who wanted to bring the truth to the Court as seen from the working classes, who fails in his bid to be a poet for the Court and to speak the truth. Because Bottom takes over the action, and he gives Theseus the opportunity, 'Will it please you to see the epilogue, or to hear a Bergomask dance between two of our company?' and of course Theseus chooses the dance, and the idiotic dance is the end. Quince disappears, and he has to go away because he has failed to tell the truth about the life of the Court, about life generally.

RB But what was the truth of the message that Quince wished to deliver to the Court?

KS I think it's a secret, but not such a secret! But the secret would be that he would say that every human feeling can be corrupted by state power. He never comes to this point in the play: they all disappear, and the actors are very happy, because they were applauded by the Court. The only man whose tragedy it is is the one who wrote the play that could never come to the Epilogue. He showed a fragment of action, a kind of analogue, a story of what happened in the Court in the four preceding Acts, but he could never speak the final position, which is what he thinks about this kind of world.

RB Can you elaborate the importance of this message that Quince is trying to get over, and particularly why it bears upon the whole theme of state power?

KS Look, Quince is to my mind very well informed as to what is going on in the Court. He knows about the two couples, and he constructs a play from real facts which are happening in the Court — people must have known them, so he knew. He constructs a play, from known facts, which would have something to do with reality. The reality of the Court concerns couples, and he has turned two couples into one couple. When he mentions Helen and Limander instead of Hero and Lysander, the association immediately comes

out, and he is clearly talking about the Court story which happened
two nights previously. Now, all these young people are present and are
watching this play, and Theseus understands immediately that he is
talking about what has happened in the Court. And he respects it,
until the point when he has to compare it with the opinion of the
young people about themselves, because they are already corrupted,
having arrived at this point in their career at Court. They believe they
are happy, they are brought by Nature together, and we know that it
is not quite like that. And there is Hippolyta. She is not full of
understanding, she wishes to punish the people for going too far, but
Theseus allows them to go on telling their story of the events at Court.
Until the point when Quince wants to tell the truth in the Epilogue,
and Bottom, being let's say a rather corrupted actor who cares much
more for his career than for the message he has to deliver, gives
Theseus his chance to choose the Bergomask instead of the Epilogue.
It is a tragic exit for Quince. He did not come to the last words he
wished to speak, because the action had taken over and the actors had
taken over the message he wanted to deliver, the truth that he
believed in and had wanted to say in his old age (thus I cast him); and
he was allowed only to dance an idiotic dance in the end. And the
Court applauds, because a dance is a solution for every situation —
much more than an Epilogue is.

   RB In a profound sense, then, the play scene in *A Midsummer
Night's Dream* is an anticipation of the play-within-a-play scene, the
Mousetrap scene, in *Hamlet*, in that both scenes are really designed to
elicit a certain response from the head of the government.

   KS I think that it is a great invention of Shakespeare's, his
creation of theatre scenes like that, bound to the basic design of the
play, and I think that there is no real difference here between *Hamlet*
and *A Midsummer Night's Dream*. His great invention is to compare
life with the stage. It touches on so many levels simultaneously, by
which you can discover that theatre-in-theatre, life-within-life, cannot
come to the ultimate point.

   RB One further point arising from your *Midsummer Night's Dream*.
It is a classic instance of the difficulties confronting the director in a
Shakespeare text: what does a fairy look like? What did your fairies
look like, and what did they represent?

   KS In the beginning I tried to find a kind of Polish fairy, which
does exist, but is very Romantic, mostly from the early nineteenth
century. But then I looked for another solution. There is a dress of
Queen Elizabeth which shows her like a snake, wise enough like a

human eye, hearing everything, having ears, and being able to say everything, having a mouth. So finally we decided to make fairies like a kind of, let's say, supporting parts, like a police of the biological kingdom, where there is an eye, where there is an ear, and there is somebody who is smiling, manufacturing a good atmosphere for the Queen. And we just used the biological parts of the human being in order to support the Queen. I did the same to Oberon with the difference that he has got his eye, he has got his smiling boy and everything like a part of the biological human being working for this kind of Court. Now there is a big difference between Puck and the fairies from Titania's train, because the other fairies believe that serving their lady, Titania, is an act of homage and self-fulfilment, while Puck believes that by participating in everything he is much better than Titania's train. And – it's my invention, but there's no other good way of showing it – this Court of Titania and Oberon is surrounded by pieces of human sensuality, listening, looking, serving, and whatever servants do in different Courts.

RB So you see the Court of Titania as being the mirror image of the Court of Theseus? And generally, in fact, the Court would appear to be the grand image of Shakespeare's work that excites your imagination.

KS For several years, because this Court was much closer to Bosch than it has ever been to any other Romantic nineteenth-century version. It had nothing to do with Goethe's imagination about the Romantic work. It became very biological, and it was done by people who were perfect in body movement, because there is a special school we have here for physical training. They are all going to be sports teachers, but they have exercises in pantomime and in classical dance. So they are able to do everything, they somehow lose their bodily weight and become extraordinarily light and graceful in their actions, moving and behaving unlike normal human beings. They are very good sportsmen, very good dancers, very expert in pantomime.

Now, what about the fairies? I think the fairies, like the Christian angels, are sexless. They are completely fulfilled in serving somebody, they are much better at that than in living their own lives. The one servant, Puck, who is not completely sexless, is a personality who understands human relationships. Somehow he is sexless, because he cannot have the relationship between a woman and a man – he can participate, like a voyeur, but his greatest opportunity is to have the power of mixing up human relationships and he enjoys it, because this brings him closer to human nature, it gives him the satisfaction of

feeling that he's not completely out of this world. It takes every kind
of mixture in human nature to satisfy him, because he's a mixture of
an unfulfilled human being, and a kind of human fantasy. His satisfaction is that everything that goes wrong in human affairs, against
human nature, brings his existence closer to the existence of human
beings. We have a kind of parallel story. The Polish devils are like that
– maybe there's no general definition of a devil, but still it's a feature
of the Devil that he mixes up every extreme human situation in order
to be supported, for his existence to be respected in this world.

RB How did you stage the final scene of *A Midsummer Night's
Dream*?

KS As a kind of promise. Because 'give me your hands' does not
mean only 'please applaud', or 'we will be in harmony with you.' It
can also be a promise for the future: when you applaud, we will tell
you in future the whole truth of what we believe about the world.
For many years, 'give me your hands' has been staged in my country
like 'be with us' or something, or the actors will even give the audience
their hands; but I think that what he promises to say is a part of his
truth, meaning that if you applaud us now, on the next occasion we
will tell you much more of the truth. I think it is a kind of false
understanding, or playing a game with the audience; when you
applaud today's truth, tomorrow will be worse and better. And I think
that's the double meaning of it.

RB And how did you project this concept in your staging?

KS A Court is not only the Prince and the Princess, the Court
consists of courtiers and people who manage affairs there. Now, I did
All's Well first, which had these two brothers Dumain, so I invented
two people whose function is to take care of the Court, so that
whenever the Court appeared they had to check if everything was OK.
They were two actors who went through the whole play without a
single line. Well, they were checking that nobody was around who
could disturb the audition of the Court, and finally when Puck was
having his last monologue they felt something, they sensed that somebody was present about the Court, invisible to them, but still
behaving on stage. They tried to catch this spirit, because they understood his lines but couldn't see him. At the last moment, when Puck
speaks his monologue, they were trying to catch him, but as he was
invisible they just caught each other's own hands. Puck disappeared
without being seen – he just made himself small and disappeared
between their legs. So they caught each other and they had to look at
each other – what is the meaning of the words? – and they were

looking around for him, and of course the audience was applauding after he'd asked them for applause. They were left without any solution, looking at each other — who is guilty? — and why do the people applaud? — as the curtain was falling.

RB So the air is filled with disturbing questions at your conclusion. Perhaps we can consider now the general questions of fidelity to Shakespeare's text and the considerations as a director, that you have in mind when you approach a Shakespeare text. Perhaps the first consideration for you, naturally, is the particular translation that you use?

KS We have quite a long tradition of Shakespeare in Poland, and the best translations — they're not adaptations — are from the late nineteenth and early twentieth centuries. These people were at least faithful to Shakespeare's text; even when they hated the plays I've been telling you about, they were faithful to the greatness of the playwright. Then we have many translations from the 1920s and 1930s and the post-war period. They mostly try to adapt Shakespeare for a modern audience, without understanding the real meaning of the lines. It is a very vulgar business, because in the end they are taking the money, and I have the feeling — when Dürrenmatt is adapting *King John*, for instance — that they make it simple for the vulgar bourgeois audience of today, in order to be understood. I think a part of the truth of Shakespeare is in between the lines, it's not in the words. And it is very vulgar to turn it into lines, and to take money for that. I even hate — you might not agree with this — Bond's adaptations because I think it is something horrible, idiots writing for idiots. When you discover what is *under* the lines of Shakespeare, and when you go deeper and try to compare your world with the world of Shakespeare, you don't need new lines.

RB Do you cut the text much?

KS No, never. I've cut maybe 10-12 lines of *All's Well*; and in *A Midsummer Night's Dream* I cut, in rehearsal, I think four jokes in the fifth Act which don't work any more. But there were only a few lines I've cut.

RB That would be considered extraordinary fidelity to the text in England and America. What other Shakespeare plays would you especially like to direct in the future?

KS It always depends on the availability of the right cast. But the next play I would like to do is *Troilus and Cressida*, because I once started it, in Germany, and I gave up because I didn't have the cast for it. Then I would very much like to do *The Tempest*, but I still don't have the cast in my theatre in Krakow. Maybe in the future I can assemble the cast in another theatre, or invite actors to this theatre to do it. I would like to repeat *Hamlet*, which I did ten years ago in Israel, to make it under Polish conditions. I like many other plays as well! But I am bound to the people I am working with, so I can only choose the plays I can really cast, and that's very difficult. I wouldn't do, say, *The Merchant of Venice* without the cast, and I don't have the cast here. But there are many other plays, many tragedies, that I would like to do.

RB It seems to me entirely logical that after your special concern with the problem plays, or the plays that relate to the problem plays, you should wish to direct *Troilus and Cressida, Hamlet*, and *The Tempest*, which are in the profoundest sense representative of the problems in Shakespeare.

TREVOR NUNN

Ralph Berry Can I ask you first about the general considerations that relate to the production of Shakespeare by the Royal Shakespeare Company?

Trevor Nunn The Royal Shakespeare Company works under a charter which demands that we should present the works of William Shakespeare at Stratford-upon-Avon. It doesn't actually state that we should present exclusively the works of William Shakespeare, but clearly the endowments that have contributed to the theatre's past and the subsidy that now contributes to the theatre's present welfare are really based on that one single directive. We are dedicated to the works of Shakespeare. To put it in a slightly livelier way, Shakespeare is our house dramatist. It's obvious that while such an instruction provides a great focus in our lives as artists, it also presents great limitations. Shakespeare wrote 37 plays, perhaps had a hand in a few more. A theatre company operating in a market town requires to do five or six plays a year in order to keep a high level of box office turnover, which argues that we need to be going through the canon once every five or six years. But of course there are certain plays that are immensely difficult to re-do that regularly; it's also true to say that there are certain plays in the canon that aren't worth doing that regularly.

Now, up to twelve years ago, when Peter Hall changed the Stratford Memorial Theatre Company into the Royal Shakespeare Company, the commitment in Stratford was largely a 'Festival Theatre' commitment. It was acknowledged that each year there should be some celebration of the bard, and audiences arrived in Stratford very much as if they were on a pilgrimage. Peter Hall's intention was to make Shakespeare live again, and therefore it was vital that the word 'Memorial' was removed from the title. The sense of that theatre being a temple, hallowed, sacrosanct, demanding awed and religious response on the part of all who entered it, was anathema to Peter. And therefore he insisted upon one simple rule: that whenever the Company did a play by Shakespeare, they should do it because the play was relevant, because the play made some demand upon our current attention. Obviously there's a great danger that the demand for a play to be 'relevant' very quickly becomes a demand that the play should be topical. Nevertheless he urged us all to consider each of the plays in the canon as if that morning it had dropped through the letterbox on to the front door mat: and therefore, what had the play got to say, that very day. This was an approach which I personally found immensely refreshing and important. In fact, I first heard Peter Hall talking about presenting the plays of Shakespeare when he came to Cambridge to do an annual lecture in the Senate House. I just happened to be passing the place — I dropped into the back row — and heard his theories of how he intended to run the theatre in Stratford, and how he would like another auditorium in London, and it all made a tremendous amount of sense to me. You see, the London auditorium is a further expression of that basic artistic stance, that is, for a company of actors to present Shakespeare's plays relevantly and vigorously, they need not only to be immensely skilled, but they need to be influenced by the writers of their own age, they must experience the influences of both ends of the writing spectrum. That is a cardinal belief the Company still holds. We still present new works and other classic plays in London, which are performed by the same actors who in alternate years go to Stratford and perform the Shakespeare plays. But here is the rub. To present the plays of Shakespeare relevantly, but also to present them (roughly) once every five or six years is contradictory. It really is that central contradiction, that pressure, which I find most difficult, and I think my colleagues find most difficult.

RB I wonder if you could elaborate that point. What is the particular difficulty about the five-year period — why is this an internal contradiction for you?

TN Well, let me give a few examples. When we did the production of *Henry V*, which came at the end of *The Wars of the Roses* sequence, recent productions of the play were still expressing a jingoistic patriotism which had been relevant to the immediate post-war situation. In fact my first contact with the play led me to believe that it was the National Anthem in five acts. The production that we did in 1964 in the midst of the 'make love not war' movements and the horror of the Vietnamese situation growing in intensity was a production which saw a play-within-a-play, a hidden play which amounted to a passionate cry by the dramatist against war. The scenes with the Archbishop of Canterbury at the beginning were presented as scenes of political cynicism.

RB Which they are, of course.

TN But which they had not previously been, or not in productions which I had seen. I think our production pointed to a disparity between the role of the Chorus and the events actually contained within the play itself. It showed us the Chorus as an Elizabethan/High Renaissance figure speaking eloquently, confirming exciting myths and fictions for an audience: the events which were then revealed in the play were very different, more real, harder, cooler, more ambiguous. Now, we haven't done a production of *Henry V* since 1964. We've revived that production, once in London, once in Stratford, but its life was finished by 1966. The difficulty that I now find is, how do we present the next play *Henry V*? I still feel very much the same things about it. However, when a play is to be presented afresh, a designer to be approached, a director and designer to work together on a concept, the play to be cast – there of course needs to be some special excitement about the project. If I were to set up, or direct a production of *Henry V* at the moment I would only wish to repeat what happened previously. Now I know that that would be no good for my colleagues, and it would probably be no good for the actors involved, and it would certainly be no good for the critics coming to see us after a number of years had elapsed. The difficulty is to avoid novelty but remain fresh. It's easy to respond to the necessity of putting a play on once every five years by saying 'It's *got* to be different, we must find a new gloss on this play, there must be a different conception from last time.' But in that way the play is done superficially, is not really considered. There are many other ways in which it's difficult to meet that five- or six-year rhythm. For instance, Peter Brook has just done a production of *A Midsummer Night's Dream* which has been so successful that I wouldn't be able to get anybody else to do a production of that play for the next ten years, even if I forced them into the theatre at gunpoint.

RB The play has been knocked out of the canon, effectively.

TN Yes. This was the case recently with *The Comedy of Errors*. In a season that I was setting up at Stratford it seemed to me that we could find another way into *The Comedy of Errors* if in presenting Shakespeare's four Roman plays we also (somewhat archly) put in *The Comedy of Errors* as Shakespeare's fifth Roman play.

RB Plautus cannot be too light.

TN In the event no one actually wished to do it, because Clifford Williams' previous version had been pretty near definitive. And consequently, after a long time, asking many directors what they might do with *The Comedy of Errors*, I arrived at the conclusion that we should do another revival, after a ten-year span, of Clifford's earlier production. Which was immensely successful. Perhaps that's an object lesson. We could revive much more of our work than we do. We tend to think of our work in the theatre in very much the way that journalists think of their work, I mean it's something to be completed, shown to the public, screwed up, and thrown away. We don't think of a production continuing to be meaningful for ten years. One part of the artistic conscience says that times have changed, society has changed, expression has changed: therefore the play must have changed. And another part says: but actually I don't think differently about it.

RB   It might be useful to think of the analogy of the old movies here. Sometimes we can watch an old movie on TV – it's thirty years old, and it's finished, it has no lasting vitality. Other thirty-year-old movies come out fresh as paint, they're good now because they were good then. They don't need re-doing. We can adapt ourselves to the conventions of thirty years ago quite easily.

TN   Yes, but of course manners and mores and morals do change radically, and the pendulum swings, and with the thirty-year-old movie it can so frequently happen that one is watching a time very similar to our own, or which seems to have a very great bearing upon our own lives. Then there are certain old movies which just show us that the artists of the time were somehow bent upon escaping and not dealing with issues. They can't interest us. The total fictions of thirty years ago are really no more interesting than the total fictions of 300 years ago, or this year.

RB   To take up the point you were making earlier though, you instanced several plays of which it seems that definitive versions have been done, for several years. But one can think of other plays in the canon that seem to have a special quality of elasticity; they are tolerant of new productions at very short intervals indeed, *Twelfth Night* for instance.

TN   Yes, obviously the most important example of such a play is *Hamlet*. It seems to me that one probably could do a production of *Hamlet* every year, a totally different production of *Hamlet* – the play that is tolerant. But there's something very special about *Hamlet*. The major character's isolation and relation to another generation is a social situation and a political situation that everybody recognises and yet it's a situation that changes from era to era. I mean, the generation gap that exists now is quite different from the generation gap that existed three years ago. There are quite different misunderstandings between parents and their children – misunderstandings, fears, aggressions have always been there, but the nature of them and how they are expressed has changed. Therefore we are bound to find

different things in that play every time we go back to it. Also it can be
a different play for every actor who plays that leading role, because
that role has got so much direct influence on the meaning of the play.
Twelfth Night is capable of many different productions, in the sense
that it is indestructible. It works even when people do appalling things
to it, like saying 'wouldn't it be a good idea to make it about a country
house society in the 1920s', or when Jonathan Miller writes a long
programme note about the neo-Platonism of the play and does a production to prove it. Actually, when all that's said and done, and we've
got over the fact that his Gemini as he called them are wandering
around with large red model dodecahedrons round their necks (having
previously assimilated that they are wearing the loose white pantaloons
of the Commedia clowns) the play survives – the human Viola and the
human Sebastian refuse to be cabined and confined by an approach
or a theory. I saw Peter Hall's production of *Twelfth Night* and its
autumnal setting and its melancholia seemed definitively right. He
had touched a Chekhov-like centre in the play; it was unarguable. And
when I saw John Barton's version of the play, it seemed to me that he
had carried Peter Hall's perception further, and in a less nineteenth-
century or operatic manner – John Barton's production was much
more stark, more of the Elizabethan playhouse – and yet, in showing
us that Belch, Aguecheek, Malvolio, Feste *and* Maria and Orsino were
all of an age who would bitterly understand 'Youth's a stuff will not
endure' he'd unlocked fully the dark and melancholic half of the play,
in contrast to which, while 'golden time convents', Viola and Olivia
and Sebastian play their games of disguise and romance. Recently it
was suggested to me that we were quite wrong to think of *Twelfth
Night* as an autumnal play: surely *Twelfth Night* is a winter play. Its
relevance to the Twelfth Night festivities was not just that it was
celebratory and joyous, but that Shakespeare clearly envisaged a bleak
deep mid-winter situation, both climatically and emotionally – a
much less funny play than tradition has made it. Immediately all
kinds of images start to emerge from the text and yet, previously,
every line of it seemed to be saying it's autumn and the leaves aren't
quite dropping off the trees, and it's watery dawns and glorious
sunsets.

RB   I think those possibilities are certainly there. Another way of
looking at it would be simply to focus on the title and point out that
Twelfth Night is really two things; it is a feast, and it is also the end to
a feast. Consequently we can take the play as being either about
revelry, or an awareness that the period of revelry is now over. And

this of course can be projected dramatically in various ways.

TN When the celebration is over Orsino has failed to learn anything
by his experience. It seems to me that while Belch and Aguecheek,
Maria and Malvolio are all pushed out into reality, Antonio is not part
of all that final celebration, he is excluded from the linking up which
dissolves the lovers into the dream world. Feste then sings that final
song, which is so urgently telling us that there may be twelve days of
celebration, but we all must arrive at the end of *Twelfth Night*, and
then what?

RB It's raining.

TN As my father always used to say when we had a few days'
holiday, 'It's back to earth tomorrow,' and he used to say it four
or five times during the final day when we were all a bit desperately
trying to enjoy ourselves. It's a strong, Puritan streak that exists in
all East Anglians. It's very important not to enjoy ourselves too much,
because of tomorrow!

RB But it was the play's statement too, I think. Malvolio would
represent that principle.

Perhaps I could ask you to focus more closely on the particular
issue that you've been talking about. We could put the question thus:
Why, in the end, do you choose a particular Shakespeare play for
production in a given season? Setting aside, obviously, certain
administrative pressures, the need to find parts for actors, the cost of
relative productions, and so forth, that we well understand.

TN Can one really set those things aside? Because they are very real
pressures, and they do very largely control the choices in any given
season. One thing that influences me very greatly in setting up a season,
is if a director has a particularly strong feeling for a play, and
(regardless of the last time it was done) if somebody is battering on my
door with furious determination to do a play I'm very well disposed
towards it. I may say that happens relatively rarely. Directors are on
the whole uncertain creatures, who require persuasion. Woo me. Woo
me. Then one has to consider who is currently in the company, whom
one would like to develop. And one has to consider whether, for a
particular play, there are any of the great actors available. You
can't embark on a *King Lear* without the certain knowledge that one
of the great actors is going to do it for you, or somebody you suspect
has greatness in him. It's a waste of everybody's time otherwise. Then
of course one has either to achieve a balance and variety in a season of
plays, or a coherence, some kind of intellectual coherence to a season.
The main examples of this would be the *Wars of the Roses* season, the

long history season of '64, the late plays season that we did in '69 and
recently the examination of the Roman plays. It's an approach that we
would like to use all the time, but of course as anyone can work out,
the number of related seasons that are possible in a collection of
thirty-seven plays is strictly limited. There are many jokes that pass
around the company, that we're going to do Shakespeare's Verona
plays, or that we're going to do Shakespeare's Early British plays . . .

RB The Roman plays are a particularly fascinating project. Why
did you want to put them on − in a group, which has never been done
before?

TN I was interested to begin with that Shakespeare should
have returned, on four separate occasions, to the same background, the
same society, and many of the same concerns for his plays. Many
people have said that *Titus Andronicus* could as well be set in
Renaissance Italy or Greece or mediaeval Britain. Its Romanness
they say is not important to it. Reading it, I found myself disagreeing.
I found that Shakespeare had made a very real attempt to surround the
events of the play with a larger social and political situation. An
empire in decline, its borders threatened by unknown and unknowable
forces, Gothic hordes. It struck me that the figure of Titus is
presented as emblematic and representative of the old Roman virtues
under attack. And it struck me that actually no other society would
have done to make the point of waning military power, moral
collapse, mockery of traditional principles and nightmarish violence
unleashed. At the beginning of the play Titus talks about his twenty-
five sons − 'half the number that King Priam had'. Now, how are we to
take such a line? First of all, it designates Titus as the emblematic
Roman military figure, the representative of a great tradition, part
myth, part real, so of course twenty-five sons, his own private army,
all of them warriors, all of them dedicated to the service of Empire
and Emperor. Secondly, one can read the line in a very naturalistic way
as an indication of character. The man maybe has had many wives,
women are totally unimportant to him and to that society, but the pro-
pagation of the family tradition is vital to him.

Of course I began to ask myself the question: How accurate was
this early picture of Rome? What did the collapse of the Roman Empire
mean to the Elizabethans? To what extent was the play post-bear-
baiting box office, and to what extent a morality play, invoking the
whole society and using Titus' story as a kind of image or parallel?
I began to see two distinct movements in the play. Shakespeare shows
us a society at breaking point, heading if not hurtling toward the cliff,

1. Jonathan Miller (Vijay)

2. *The Tempest* Jonathan Miller, Mermaid Theatre
Prospero/Graham Crowden, Caliban/Rudolph Walker
(Forbes Nelson)

3. *The Tempest* Jonathan Miller, Mermaid Theatre
Prospero/Graham Crowden, Ariel/Norman Beaton
(Forbes Nelson)

4. Konrad Swinarski (Le Théâtre en Pologne)

5. (left) *All's Well That Ends Well* Konrad Swinarski, Teatr Stary,
Krakow
Helena/Anna Polony, King of France/Marek Walczewski
(Le Théâtre en Pologne)

6. (above) *A Midsummer Night's Dream* Konrad Swinarski, Teatr Stary,
Krakow
Titania/Halina Slojewska, Bottom/Stanislaw Gronkowski
(Le Théâtre en Pologne)

7. Robin Phillips

8. (bottom left) *Measure for Measure* Robin Phillips, Stratford Festival
Theatre, Ontario
Angelo/Brian Bedford, Isabella/Martha Henry
(Robert G. Ragsdale)

9. (below) *Hamlet* Robin Phillips, Stratford Festival Theatre, Ontario
Ophelia/Marti Maraden, Claudius/Michael Liscinsky, Ophelia's Lady/
Patricia Bentley-Fisher
(Robert G. Ragsdale)

10. Peter Brook

11. (below) *Timon of Athens* Peter
Brook, Théâtre des Bouffes-du-Nord,
Paris
Timon/François Marthouret
(Béatrice Heylisers)

12. (right) *Timon of Athens* Peter Brook
Brook, Théâtre des Bouffes-du-Nord,
Paris
Timon/François Marthouret
(Nicolas Treatt)

13. Trevor Nunn (Reg Wilson)

14. *Julius Caesar* Trevor Nunn, Royal
Shakespeare Theatre
Cassius/Patrick Stewart, Brutus/John
Wood, Caesar/Mark Dignam
(Reg Wilson)

15. *Coriolanus* Trevor Nunn, Royal Shakespeare Theatre
(Joe Cocks)

16. Michael Kahn (Martha Swope)

17; (bottom left) *Romeo and Juliet* Michael Kahn, American
Shakespeare Theater, Stratford, Conn.
Juliet/Roberta Maxwell, Paris/Donald Warfield, Nurse/Kate Reid
(Martha Swope)

18. (below) *Love's Labour's Lost* Michael Kahn, American
Shakespeare Theater, Stratford, Conn.
King of Navarre/Charles Siebert, Berowne/Lawrence Pressman
(Friedman-Abeles)

19. Giorgio Strehler (Mario Mulas)

20. *Das Speil Der Machtigen* Giorgio Strehler
(Luigi Ciminaghi)

21. *King Lear* Giorgio Strehler
Lear/Tino Carraro
(Luigi Ciminaghi)

as the rigidity and discipline of a great past is thrown aside, reviled and mocked. But secondly he shows us just how damaging are those rigid disciplinarian principles when (to be upheld) they override a man's human instinctive responses. Blinkered Titus kills his own son for a principle, refuses to bury him for a principle, gives away his daughter for a principle and accepts the execution of two other sons on principle. His awakening from a disciplinarian past is painful and moving, and, as in *Lear* later on, the old man cannot cope and loses his treasured reason. It was when reading that play that I was struck by the entrance of Aemilius, who says to the gibbering Saturninus that Lucius is heading towards Rome with an army of Goths, who threatens to do more for his revenge than Coriolanus ever did. And I suddenly thought, how current was the Coriolanus myth? Who was interested in that story when Shakespeare was writing *Titus Andronicus*? Who in his audience would have understood it? Where did Shakespeare get it from? If he was picturing the collapse of Rome, into a wilderness of tigers, into a brutal vengeful collection of animals, and here is referring to a little known incident about the very beginnings of Rome, what was forming in his mind, and what did he make of it? And really, from that beginning, I started to re-examine the three plays, *Julius Caesar, Antony and Cleopatra* and *Coriolanus*, acknowledging of course that there is a superficial relationship between *Julius Caesar* and *Antony and Cleopatra* because they share some of the same characters, but they're written in very different styles. It occurred to me more and more that Shakespeare seemed to be finding, by using the Roman background, Roman imagery, the opportunity to make free comment about political issues he just wasn't able to when writing the English history plays. There was always the overriding factor of having to support the Tudor dynasty, though of course the kind of true king/ false king arguments that run through these plays is fascinating. Nevertheless, there clearly is no *freedom* for the dramatist to express himself, and in the Roman plays he does go much further. Now Shakespeare, like all great dramatists, finds it impossible to write about a character other than from the point of view of that character, and consequently he's no propagandist. And I certainly didn't do these plays to try to prove that Shakespeare was in any sense presenting finished and coherent political conclusions.

RB I think there are really two theses here, which I personally find very convincing. One is that Shakespeare's plays are among other things dramatic notebooks, in which he alludes in code form, if you like, to unwritten plays he's going to get around to later. Your

Coriolanus reference in *Titus Andronicus* seems to me a persuasive example of this. And the other thesis is that Shakespeare has a certain idea of Rome that remains, very broadly, a constant in his life, and Rome is among other things a way of writing about political problems in such a way that they are virtually free from censorship, they are not taken (perhaps) to allude to contemporary England.

TN Having started on this line of enquiry, I wanted to present just the three plays, *Julius Caesar, Antony and Cleopatra* and *Coriolanus*, insisting of course that there was no special chronological significance about them, there was nothing of the history cycle in them. But it seemed to me that it was a great shame not to examine *Titus Andronicus* again too, so I decided to do all four, really in a manner of open enquiry. I was not expecting to find clear relationships between them, but I wanted myself and the actors to *find out*. It seemed to me that it would be a pretty dry and academic exercise to take the plays in the order in which they were written. That couldn't have had a great deal of interest for the actors — they had to believe in the real situations in which they were involved, not the literary relationships, and consequently for them to feel that there was some kind of historical connection between the plays was, I think, a good and productive thing for them. They did a great deal of background work which I think helped the plays in performance. Of course it's inevitable that, having presented the plays in one season, there should be comparison with the *Wars of the Roses* sequence, although no comparison is possible.

RB Essentially, the *Wars of the Roses* forms a narrative, and the Roman plays, whatever else they are, are not a narrative. They are ways of opening out, spatially, areas of political action and conduct.

TN Yes. Of course, they all introduce the theme of the disparity and friction between private and public. I mean, private morality and public necessity. I think the biggest contribution that we made in doing the plays was to reveal more of the character of Brutus and the position of *Julius Caesar* in Shakespeare's development. I began to understand that it was much more closely related to *Hamlet* than I had previously reckoned — to realise that Brutus was faced with the problem of assassinating his best friend and therefore has to make a moral/ political choice.

RB I found your *Julius Caesar* startlingly original in at least two major ways, in terms of character presentation. Your Caesar was the first I've ever seen who's really struck me as being dangerous, an enemy to the state. Every other Caesar has appeared to me as a sort of company chairman, who's a little bit over the top, and the Board are getting rather restive about him. He doesn't really seem that much of a problem. He does in your production. And the other is Brutus. Every other production I've seen takes at face value the adjective that is applied to him constantly throughout the play, 'the noble Brutus'. Your production questions this. And taken together, this sheds a flood of light on the play for me.

TN Yes. Brutus himself questions his nobility. He questions himself and his own actions constantly. When at the height of the tent scene Brutus turns on Cassius and says, 'I shall be glad to learn of *noble* men', it's a vicious taunt at Cassius, but I also think it's an indication of the self-revulsion that is in him. We were able to find a complete continuity for the character by questioning that endlessly repeated adjective. Viewed through Cassius' (myopic) eyes, Caesar is fundamentally *ignoble* in wishing to retain and consolidate power. The aristocratic tradition is otherwise, a commitment to preserve the idea of equality and freedom — as John Wood (who played Brutus) once pointed out, freedom for Cassius to dislike Caesar publicly without fear of arrest. Both Brutus and Cassius die amidst uncertainty, but they know that a whole era has come to an end. 'It is *impossible* that Rome shall ever breed thy fellow' — because Rome has changed. 'Our day is gone,' says Titinius. The opportunists and Empire builders have taken over. So far as Caesar is concerned — I was reading recently a review by Bernard Crick who, writing about the plays, lamented that we had chosen a simple and naïve Mussolini-like solution for the character, and pointed out that the problem Shakespeare is dealing with is less obvious than that. It seems to me he has put his finger on the difficulty with the play in performance. If one *doesn't* suggest that Caesar is fast becoming a military dictator — I mean, that after the civil war he has total control of the army, and therefore cannot be removed — he can't be *voted* out, and he's not going to move over, to let somebody else enjoy that power he has fought for — if one doesn't suggest that military power supports him, and if he doesn't in some way embody that military power, then obviously we get to the moment of his assassination and we just think that it's dreadfully unfair and dreadfully unnecessary that so many people should set upon a harmless defenceless senator.

There's a great deal of evidence in the play that Caesar has reached a point of dangerous insanity. Not only the number of times that he refers to himself in the third person, and as an institution, not only in the terrifying 'Northern Star' speech just before the assassination, but

in little references like from Casca, 'there was more foolery yet . . .'
What happens to the two tribunes? This is something that I haven't
picked up in any previous production – maybe that's because I wasn't
concentrating – but Casca says that Marullus and Flavius, the tribunes
of the people, 'for pulling scarfs off Caesar's images, are put to silence.'
Surely he means they've been executed. It's been very sudden. Two
men in high office have been executed and all they did was to pull
down a decoration off an image which until last year no one was
allowed to put up in the first place. Now that's deeply sinister and
deeply disturbing, the cult of the individual leader has arrived, Fascist
control has happened. It can be argued that it's a tiny reference to it,
but I believe that what Shakespeare is trying to do at the moment is
to suggest that these things cannot be *openly* discussed; and why
Brutus has to pluck Casca by the sleeve, is because it is no longer
possible to go openly up to Casca and say, 'Hey, what just happened?'
It has to be secret, cloak and dagger. A police state is either in existence
or is imminent, everybody is going to report on everybody else. Can
Cassius trust Brutus, who after all when the play begins is a chief
adviser to the supremo? Can Casca be trusted? Where does Artemidorus
get his information from? So I think one *has* to be that graphic in a
stage production. On the other hand we did try very hard to show
Caesar's humanity – wherever it exists in the text. Again, it seems to
me it's not Shakespeare's primary concern – at the beginning of the
play we tried to present a relationship with Antony from the little
suggestions of 'you and I like plays and Cassius doesn't' or 'you and I
laugh a lot and Cassius doesn't', but actually there are no opportunities
in the play for Caesar to laugh a lot. He's constantly disturbed by
soothsayers, by prophecies and by premonitions of one sort or
another, he is decidedly unrelaxed, fainting, angry, disputatious.

RB You worked in too that nice line that Jonson reports, 'Caesar
did never wrong, but with just cause.'

TN I'm sure that's the original. If one does take that to be the
line, it's the ultimate statement of the power-obsessed dictator. Papal
infallibility, etc.

RB I'm glad you replaced that line. It was too good to be taken
out just because Jonson laughed at it.

TN I get the feeling that something like that must have happened.

RB And *Coriolanus*?

TN *Coriolanus* really is my favourite play, and I am annoyed that
I can't get it as clear and as good in performance as I want it. Here is
the example of the mature Shakespeare adopting every possible point

of view through his characters, approving of nobody, but rejecting nobody — and so allowing a complex debate to occur.

RB How did your actors experience the problems of the Roman plays? How did they react to the text and its difficulties? What did you find to be the major difficulties at the rehearsal stage?

TN We began in ideal circumstances. We had a four-week period in London with a totally available company which is rare, a large bare rehearsal room, and no restrictions on the scheduling of rehearsals or undue pressures of time. So we talked and we improvised a great deal. We improvised every single situation in *Coriolanus*, we improvised a lot of *Julius Caesar*, nothing more memorably than the assassination. I only wish I could have recaptured what happened in the rehearsal room when some of the actors were using texts and some of the actors, overwhelmed, were using the only words that occurred to them at the moment.

RB If I can speak as a member of the audience here, something special unquestionably did come through. What was particularly powerful about the assassination as you staged it was that the emotional effect came after the killing, rather than the event itself. The reactions of the assassins to the deed that they had done was the most powerful stroke of theatre.

TN That's exactly what happened at the improvisation. The incident was quick, many people had no time to move, and some people genuinely thought that some joke was being played. We discovered why it could be possible for the senate area to be surrounded by guards, yet for none of them to prevent the killing. The four guards were positioned quite close to Caesar. They had been told that their job on which their lives depended was to prevent any harm happening to Caesar at any time, but they still didn't move. We conducted a series of interviews after the event to try to find out from people, as it would be TV reporters trying to find out; what did they feel? What happened? Give us your version. And the guards were agreed that it wasn't their place to go into the middle of the Senate floor. That's where the politicians went, that's where the great speeches were given. Whatever happened there, it was not for them to interfere. But then we also discovered that once the assassination had happened, there was a long, stunned time, when nobody said or felt anything. Then there was pandemonium, which of course is exactly noted in the text. Shakespeare's naturalistic writing amazes me. He is so accurate. In improvisation John Wood desperately required to be able to say to everybody, 'stand still', he needed to impose some order or pattern. And then contradictorily, he had the feeling that everybody else must go away, for the double reason that the responsible people must now deal with the immediate aftermath, and if people were going to get hurt it should be himself and his colleagues and not innocent people. In the improvisation it became absolutely clear how different the assassins' attitudes were. Cassius just couldn't stop stabbing at Caesar. That's a much more emotive part of the improvisation process, but since there is more of a personal vendetta between Cassius and Caesar — this was the moment when it really got expressed. Cassius was crazed, frenzied, and Brutus stopped him. In the tent scene Cassius threatens Brutus, with 'I may do that I shall be sorry for' and Brutus replies, 'You have done that you should be sorry for.' That always seemed to us to be a paralysing moment. Brutus is talking about the assassination, and what Cassius has revealed of his motives. I am not saying that is unarguably the meaning of the line, but in performance it could only mean that one thing to the actors.

RB These improvisations that you practise are obviously superbly effective at bringing out the inner truth of the lines, the energies of the drama if you like. How did you deal with the more obviously technical problems of the text — I think of matters like verse/prose distinctions, and the like?

TN In the Royal Shakespeare Company, we're very fortunate in having John Barton, who is a Shakespeare scholar, and who is specially talented in teaching actors and helping actors with difficult texts. Consequently, at the beginning of rehearsals for the Roman plays, we had verse classes and a great deal of Barton-led text work. Our attitude to the text has to vary from play to play, as Shakespeare's language varies from play to play — sometimes our attitude has to vary from scene to scene, because Shakespeare's language varies from scene to scene. We mustn't *generalise*. The modern actor confronted with a complex Shakespearian text generalises. He tries to suck out its emotional meaning; he re-presents the text with a generalised colouring of the words which he believes will somehow communicate that emotional meaning. And he won't be specific, he won't coin language at the very moment when it is emotionally necessary. I have done some work with a remarkable voice teacher called Kristen Linklater. Her most eloquent instruction is 'Don't colour the words; let the words colour you.' But 'letting' or 'allowing' is the most difficult process for an actor. It takes such a long time, and such a lot of trust. The only satisfactory approach that I have ever found with a difficult text is to

start with the totally naturalistic situation. To work at communicating
that situation until language of greater complexity becomes necessary.
Until the full text that Shakespeare has provided becomes necessary.
No words must be superfluous. Or decorative. What we do invariably
with our actors these days is to work with Shakespeare sonnets. That
highly organised, compressed speech presents every possible language
problem, breathing problem and technical problem to an actor. But
equally, none of the sonnets will work unless it communicates a
human situation, particula r, felt and experienced. Therefore each
sonnet must be personalised, and we challenge the actors to find the
situation which would provide this expression, this language. We ask,
who is it about, who are you talking to, in your own words what
happened? We find in matters of phrasing, in matters of timing, in
matters of feeling, the sonnet insists that the speaker doesn't generalise,
so many different changes of tone and meaning occur within its short
length. We discover that an actor very quickly gets a sense of how to
use a rhyme, like a concluding couplet, because the rhyme is necessary
to support some sense of finality, or uplift, or plangent melancholy; but
because the rhyme is necessary, it must be acknowledged, it must be
used. Now, though I say our text work varies from play to play, we do
intensive work on sonnets at the beginning of each season, and we also
have poetry classes organised by our voice teacher Cis Berry.

With *Coriolanus*, I found myself encouraging the actors to forget
about the formal demands of the text altogether, to treat the
Coriolanus text only as naturalistic speech; Shakespeare anyway comes
closer in this play to naturalistic speech than in any other; first of all
because of the amount of prose that exists in the play (the citizen
text, the officers, Adrian and Nicenor, and so on) but also because of
the particular quality of the verse. It is deliberately irregular, lame or
long. It reads like well-organised, though tightly compressed, prose.
It would be disastrous for the actors to try to regularise it, by marking
each line ending, or pausing to preserve a pentameter beat, because
actually what Shakespeare is doing is to work against the pentameter,
to provide (especially for his trained audience, attuned to the pentameter) the effect of natural rhythms.

RB It's curious, isn't it, that here is a play commonly regarded as
an extreme instance, in drama, of the class conflict, and yet you are
saying that the prose/verse distinctions (with all that they imply) are
perhaps less emphatic here.

TN I'm saying in *Coriolanus* the verse looks after itself. If it's not
heavily marked — and you can't take an end-of-line pause in most of

that verse, you just can't do it — you've got to follow its punctuation, its sense. It's surprisingly spare, it's the language of political debate and argument. Of course we are aware that the patricians are speaking a heightened speech, an organised speech, a highly selected speech, and that the plebeians are not. We are also aware that the tribunes are speaking aristocratic speech, which is beautifully judged by Shakespeare. But in that play I encouraged people not to get hung up on the text. I asked them to learn it with total accuracy — it's not a text that's going to look after itself if it's at all sloppily rendered. Whereas in *Caesar* I demanded that the speaking of the text was very disciplined, very strongly marked, and that time and again the end of the line was important to the meaning of the line, important to the next phrase. Oh, yes, *Caesar* is very different from *Coriolanus*. Just look at it on the page. For *Antony and Cleopatra* which is so rich, so blown, we did a great deal of work with Kristen Linklater, the voice teacher. We did some peculiar improvisations, like trying to express colours with sounds, and then colours with words — very tactile use of sounds. I really wanted the actors to relish everything of the *Antony* text, to relish it like they were eating it. It's something quite sumptuous and succulent. I wanted the actors to be reluctant to let each phrase go. We didn't achieve all we set out to but we were on the right track. I really do think that the demands of the plays vary: work that one would do on *Love's Labour's Lost* would be totally different from anything one would say to a group of actors doing, say, *Henry IV Part Two*.

    RB This is a matter of the most piercing judgement and sensibility, this central decision as to what is the quality of the language of a given play that one ought to reach towards, and then embody this quality so far as one can judge it in one's production.

    TN It was terribly clear to me, in *The Revenger's Tragedy*, that the language is brittle and flinty and sharp and jagged and consonantal; all the work that we did was towards that. Voice classes used to go on where literally all speech was consonants, and everybody's jaws were made to work overtime. Sometimes I got people to render certain sections in French, because in French you have to use consonants more, you have to be more precise. I was also trying to reveal things of the tone of the play, people being vicious towards each other, cynical, mocking, hurtful to each other. I think a good deal of that communicated.

    The text that I didn't trust, and should have trusted, was *Much Ado About Nothing*. I tried to overorganise the actors in those great flowing

prose sections of the play, I tried to show them that there were all
kinds of rhythmic things that were happening within their speeches,
and I think that I made something too artificial of the play. Instead of
trusting its rhythms, I emphasised and demonstrated them.

RB I think that perhaps the difficulty with *Much Ado* is that there
are not only several plots in that play, but that the plots come from
different plays. And the characters speak a language which is on a
different level. I am thinking especially of Claudio and Hero, who are
really inhabiting a quite different world from Benedick and Beatrice.
It's not one of the plays in which the language appears totally to
envelop, uniformly, everybody in the play, as in *Romeo and Juliet* or
the Roman plays.

TN The language of Claudio and Hero and (on certain occasions)
of Don Pedro expresses a naïveté, a blinkered, romantic self-indulgence
and that didn't sufficiently emerge in the version of the play that I
did (on either occasion) because I tried to overorganise the prose.
Actually the language of the play gets more difficult as it progresses,
as the comedy becomes blacker — I have yet to see the play done with
sufficient seriousness. 'Kill Claudio' is for real. Claudio's penance at the
tomb mustn't be undervalued.

RB Could we think about textual matters generally, and your
approach to cutting? What are your general thoughts about a Shakespeare text, as it comes to you?

TN 'The two hours' traffic of our stage . . .' Cutting is always a
dreadful thing to have to do, but I haven't done a *complete* Shakespeare
play yet. The first production I ever did was *Hamlet* when I was 18,
and I only cut about 50 lines. But then it ran for five hours. Peter
Brook only cut about ten lines of *A Midsummer Night's Dream*, I think
I only cut about twenty lines of *Julius Caesar*. When you approach the
text of *Hamlet*, the cutting virtually is the production. What you decide
to leave in is your version of the play.

RB So the question is not, do you cut, but: which play are you
going to present?

TN Oh yes, in *Hamlet* that's certainly so. And, to an extent in
Lear. There's so much that has to be left out. I did a production of
Lear that lasted for four hours and ten minutes, and I still regretfully
had to take masses of the play out. Which leads me to suppose that the
versions of the play that we now have don't necessarily represent
playing versions. I don't think that everything was played in the
Elizabethan theatre. We have discovered when we do a certain kind
of rehearsal, running a scene very fast in order to get the actors' minds

really tuned and their responses more flexible, that it's possible to play a Shakespeare text much faster than we usually do in performance. One is bombarded with words, one ends up by understanding what is going on. One feels replete, but one just hasn't concentrated on any of the details. Like speed reading I suppose. So I sometimes wonder whether what's changed most of all in four hundred years is the speed of the playing. I really do think that if we went back in the proverbial time-machine and saw Burbadge and Co., we wouldn't understand a word of what they were talking about.

RB Because they would be talking so rapidly?

TN And in a dialect that would distort the language to a degree much more than for instance a Geordie does in present-day English. I'm sure that when Burbadge talked about 'the dogs of *waahr*' and 'put up your bright *sworrds*, for the dew will rust them,' it would have been physically and musically thrilling – much more onomatopoeic, much more expressive than our present speech. We were talking about cutting, though. Not only do I think cutting necessary, but (unfortunately) it can become extremely enjoyable: the study exercise of making a slightly different scene from the one that exists on the page by linking certain speeches together or leaving a section out is most seductive. Occasionally what is required is a line here or two lines there, in order to make sense of a passage. So one has to write the line or two. That too is a wickedly enjoyable exercise. And nobody ever, ever notices.

RB Cutting, I suppose, highlights the central problem of fidelity to Shakespeare's text. What do you think of as fidelity to Shakespeare's text – if indeed this can be usefully defined, or described at all?

TN There is an approach to directing Shakespeare which is exemplified in the phrase, 'wouldn't it be a good idea if . . .', and that approach upsets me. Any production of a Shakespeare play that I do, or my colleagues do, must start with the text. It must start with combing that text for its imagery, for its central ideas, for its visual ideas, and therefore I disdain the quick reading of the play which produces the superficial thought, 'this would work excellently as a Regency melodrama', 'this would be extremely pointed if we did it as a Chicago gangster show.' In that sense my loyalty to the text is total, because it is my starting point and my finishing point. But I am not a fundamentalist about the text, because my prime concern *must* be to make the plays work in a theatre to an audience living now. Therefore if I have to make cuts, if I have to make elisions, if I have to telescope, even – dare I say it – in certain limited circumstances, expand, I will do so. The *Wars of the Roses* is an excellent case in point, because it seems to me that *Henry VI Parts One, Two* and *Three*, and *Richard III* on four consecutive evenings would be a very gruelling experience. John Barton transposed, brought in sections of other plays, and in making the cuts and transpositions wrote certain sections himself. He has been totally honest about it, and has published the result, and it's a fascinating document, it shows what happens to plays once they get into the playhouse, and are amended and reshaped — and reading it one gets a very clear picture of how the three or four different hands may have worked on the original. That's an extreme example of what we in the RSC are prepared to do with a text. Terry Hands did a version of *The Merry Wives of Windsor*; he put together all the quartos of the play, and I think he came up with something very remarkable. The version that he made is about to be published; he actually sorted out the two sub-plots with a clarity that hasn't happened previously. I did a certain amount of such work with *Titus Andronicus* — we did more than a certain amount in *The Revenger's Tragedy*. But in *Titus Andronicus* I included two speeches in the version by using a mixture of other Elizabethan dramatists and myself; I think they work tremendously well, because they expanded and focused certain things that are intended in the original text but are presented obliquely.

RB So your watchword then would be loyalty to the text, rather than a kind of, shall I say, meticulous adherence to the letter of it.

TN Yes. I mean, I do get disturbed when people turn up at Stratford-upon-Avon and sit in the third row of the stalls, and as the play begins they open their text and follow partly the play and partly the text. That does seem to me to be a very sad thing for anybody to do at a live performance. The play is to be experienced, not to be checked.

MICHAEL KAHN

Ralph Berry I'd like first to ask you about your work as Director of the Shakespeare Festival at Stratford.

Michael Kahn Yes, we call it the Shakespeare Theater now, not Festival, but that's not important.

RB Well, perhaps it may be important. You'll remember that the Royal Shakespeare did change their name (from Shakespeare Memorial Theatre Company) a decade ago, and they felt it was a good deal more than a face-lift.

MK I think that we felt that dropping 'Festival' was also more than just cutting out a word in our name, in that 'Festival', although it has connotations of joy, of coming together in celebration of something, which I still believe the American Shakespeare Theater should do, also has some connotations of being simply a sort of less serious, mostly summer operation. And our goal together for the AST is to move into a really year-round operation, and to mix productions of Shakespeare with modern productions and to create a company that works together for more than four or five months. And to create an audience awareness for more than four or five months. So we dropped the word 'Festival' for that reason, although I think the celebratory aspects of the Festival we still like. We kept the name 'Shakespeare'.

RB There would obviously be very general advantages in a more mixed, or balanced, programme: but specifically for Shakespeare, would you see a system producing more contemporary plays as providing an advantage, in the Shakespearian context?

MK Yes, it has been in several ways. One is I think that one's muscles, both physical and intellectual, really are different — what one uses when one approaches a Shakespeare, and a modern play — and I think that the refreshing of each of those at a given time only helps the other. And I think that the form you find in Shakespeare you can bring to a modern play, and a certain freedom you get from a modern play you can bring to Shakespeare. I think any company that only does classical plays has a tendency to atrophy in a way; because there's so much work on technique, on even the most simple things like vocal production and physical stamina, that you can sometimes forget other basic things that working on a modern piece makes you do. Or even ways of thinking: if you do a very abstract or *avant-garde* piece, it

makes you perhaps realise that certain logical ways of thinking are not
necessarily true or helpful, and so you might notice that again in
Shakespeare which you might not if you're not encountering other
materials and other minds, other ways of writing and other ways of
seeing things. I find it very healthy. With me, if I only did Shakespeare,
if I wasn't able to go off some place else at the moment and do Harold
Pinter or Sam Shepard or the kind of plays I do in the off season, I
would feel constricted in some way. I would like that experience that
I'm having personally to be the experience of the company, together,
because I would like to bring that sort of investigation to Shakespeare
and vice versa. I know that I bring to Sam Shepard a kind of appreciation of the language, a kind of scope, that perhaps another director who
doesn't do Shakespeare doesn't. And I would like to bring to Shakespeare, and with those actors together, some of those freedoms that I
know are in Shakespeare but that one is forced to use when one is with
Sam Shepard.

RB Do you find that directing Pinter has a bearing on Shakespeare?

MK Of course, when you're doing Shakespeare, you're terribly
aware of language all the time. I find that there are all those things
behind the words, and around the words; what one does physically
is important – and of course a good deal of what you communicate in
Pinter is communicated in silence, either by doing something or by not
doing something. And I think that in the productions of Shakespeare
that's probably true.

RB When you come to frame up a season's programme theatrically
there are certain administrative aspects that you have to bear in mind –
you have to make fairly sure of audience appeal, you have to work
within a budget, and find work for certain actors, and so forth . . .

MK Yes, those things are already very difficult.

RB . . . Those are large factors, obviously. But beyond those factors,
what makes you select a given Shakespeare play?

MK I've always tried never to do a play that doesn't engage me at
that particular time. And I think that some plays of Shakespeare
engage one at different times. I am more interested in some plays now
than I was five years ago, and less interested now in some plays than
five years ago. And I think that it has to do with one's relationship
to the world at that given moment, as to what concerns one the most.
I think it's very personal, and one can sense that there are times when
certain plays are really *done*. I noticed that when, for instance, I did
Julius Caesar and *Antony and Cleopatra* it was at the time when the
Royal Shakespeare Company was doing *Julius Caesar* and *Antony and*

Cleopatra in the same season. I think that's partly because both of us were interested in politics on the grand scale, and it was a very political year; actually it turned out to be an election year in the United States, and one was concerned about leadership and public images. And so, *Julius Caesar*: which is not a play that I've particularly admired before, probably because it's that play that we're all taught in America in the ninth grade and it almost finishes us for good, you know, with Shakespeare. It's a play that I've seen many times and had never had any particular desire to do it — and I felt myself absolutely fascinated by it. But then I re-read it at a time when we were in the middle of an election, and a complicated election in this country, because at the time I could find no candidate to vote for. Although my sympathies were for George McGovern I thought he would make a terrible President, and my sympathies were not for Richard Nixon but I thought he would probably make a better President than George McGovern although he was a despicable human being. I found politics to be an almost insoluble problem to deal with, and I found that to be true in *Julius Caesar*. It interested me that in *Julius Caesar* everybody was right and everybody was wrong, and I thought that was really true and became fascinated by it. And then I followed that through to *Antony and Cleopatra*, although at a certain time *Antony and Cleopatra* stops being a political play and becomes another kind of play. There are time times — there was a time when everybody was doing *The Tempest*, which was about two years ago, and I think that was because there was a sense of a mystical appeal. People were becoming involved whether they knew it or not in a sense of mysticism; although for me ritual areas of *The Tempest* are most interesting. And I honestly feel that right now everyone is going to be involved in *Lear*, this sort of cataclysmic universe, and I think that that's the play for now.

But I find that I respond very personally to plays and that sometimes (it's a little presumptuous to say this of Shakespeare) it's because a play helps say something a little more at a given moment, or, much more true of Shakespeare, a play helps you investigate something that you know is concerning you. You encounter, or have the chance to encounter in the play, a problem. I didn't think when I was doing *Julius Caesar* I was saying something about politics, but I felt in the working on it, the thinking about it, that I was beginning to deal through Shakespeare with responses to politics that at the moment were concerning me. And sometimes those other plays don't mean much any more. When I did *Love's Labour's Lost* in 1968 I was concerned with manners — we seemed to be in a time of superstars of one form or another whose fame was really based upon personality and modes of behaviour. That's not true right now, and *Love's Labour's Lost* does not interest me now. I think it's a beautiful play, but I would not be drawn to *Love's Labour's Lost* now, whereas in 1968 we were involved in the Beatles and the Onassis and the Kennedy ladies and Lee Radziwill and Mia Farrow and Truman Capote, and we had a series of pop stars and jet-setters, which I think was really the germ for Shakespeare's writing it too. It fascinated me, but it wouldn't now, because the era of media pop stars is over.

RB So not only is there a very personal feeling of commitment that you have towards a particular play at a given moment, but also it's broadly social, you feel it (in part) because it's in the air. One director I know uses the image of the barometer — he says the director is the barometer of society.

MK Well, I used to say that I was worried if I didn't have my finger on the pulse of the nation. But I don't think that's necessarily what I mean. I think yes, that's true very often. (We don't really have to define 'society'.) It is interesting that many different plays are chosen by many different companies at the same time; it never ceases to fascinate me. Then you have the many plays to pick from. And aside from commercial considerations, that is having to do the one crowd seller, the audiences still come to twelve plays more than they come to others.

RB I think there's undoubtedly a 'viable' play at any one time. For instance, everyone I've talked to would like to do a *Troilus and Cressida* (again, even).

MK Yes. I would have preferred to do *Troilus and Cressida* two years ago. I said the other day jokingly that really we didn't ought to do *Troilus and Cressida* until there's another war. And therefore I hoped that *Troilus and Cressida* was no longer a play for our time. But I would have liked the opportunity to do *Troilus and Cressida* during the Vietnam war, rather than at this period of uncertain peace that we're in now — as a warning perhaps, yes, but I think it would have been even more immediate two years ago.

RB Perhaps we could think about the phase of implementing your concept of a text. You are talking, for instance, about *Julius Caesar* as a political play, which it surely is, much more than *Antony and Cleopatra*. How did you go about implementing what you understand to be the political aspects of *Julius Caesar*?

MK Well, I must preface this by saying that there are many things that I don't do any more when I'm working on Shakespeare, that I

used to do. I no longer thought that *Julius Caesar* has a particular
point of view or that I would bring a point of view to *Julius Caesar*.
What I found interesting about *Julius Caesar* was the fact that it was
an investigation into, rather than a definition of, a situation. And so
perhaps six or seven years ago I would have concerned myself with a
decision: is Julius Caesar a Fascist, or totalitarian – what *is* he? And
maybe I'd have something to say there. Partly this has to do more
with what I'm beginning to understand about Shakespeare, that what
I really tried to do in *Julius Caesar* was to present a whole series of
paradoxes. I thought that's what politics was, simply a series of
paradoxes, and that *Julius Caesar* was both dangerous and at the same
time necessary. And I kept coming to terms with that in my own life;
a strong leader is often better than a weak leader, but a strong leader
is also dangerous. And then in *Julius Caesar* you have a dangerous man
who's a strong leader, but when he's destroyed so is the Republic.
And that is absolutely extraordinary, that's an act of courage on the
part of the writer to say that, to say that's the truth, and that Brutus,
who seems to be right, is also wrong. His intentions are right, his
intellect is right, but at the same time he fails through a series of very
foolish mistakes. Of course, at the time I could not help but think that
George McGovern and Brutus were rather similar, but I didn't any
longer say that I must make the audience know that Brutus *was* George
McGovern. As a matter of fact I was very uninterested, and thought
that if they went around thinking that Brutus was George McGovern
and Caesar was Richard Nixon, that I would have done Shakespeare a
disservice, because it would have made it another play. And so what I
tried to do was to be true to the differences between each of those
people, to try to make perfectly clear to exist side by side what was
valuable about Caesar and what was dangerous; that was the problem,
and there was no answer. It may be because I'm confused, and it may be
that I have fewer answers, but I've tried to do a production which said:
this is the problem of government and politics, that side by side exist
the weak and the strong and the good and the bad and the possible and
the impossible, and that so far we've not found an answer to that.
And of course I haven't found the answer to that in life, and I don't
think the play does either. But I sympathised in that sense with every
single character, and I thought they were all also wrong.

   RB This is a fascinating illumination into the director's problem.
But with that text, as with others, a point of decision has to be faced.
Essentially, I suppose, the decision is on this question: how do you
project the part of Julius Caesar? How dangerous is the man? Because

if he is seen to be dangerous you have resolved, or defined the problem in a certain way. If on the other hand you present him as a rather harmless old gentleman, way over the top in his career, then you have resolved the problem in another way.

MK Well, I try to do both. I must say it was rather difficult. I also thought, Antony really loves Caesar. One can say he's a playboy of the time. But he's not a fool, and he genuinely loves Caesar. So to say that Caesar is simply dangerous is to deny the fact that one of the most significant characters in the play — and when we are doing *Antony and Cleopatra* with it, therefore the most significant character because of the continuation of the two plays for that season — has his strongest affections and loyalties with Julius Caesar. So taking that as a guide, I felt, yes, he's dangerous, he's a tyrant, he's vain, he's egotistical, but at the same time he commands a genuine affection from someone whom one is expected (by Shakespeare, in a sense) to respect. And I had to come to terms with that, and I did not want to say that Antony therefore was a sort of H. R. Haldeman being just loyal to his master. I thought no, he's a bright man, and certainly bright enough, or emotional enough to deliver the oration, and keep right on going through *Antony and Cleopatra*. Caesar is dangerous, and yet at the same time he has kept Rome together, and when they kill him, Rome falls apart. And Octavius is *not* a better choice. Among other factors, the irony I suppose of doing these two plays together is that you finish up at the end of *Antony and Cleopatra* with another Julius Caesar, perhaps even more dangerous, because he's young and has marched like a machine right through *Antony and Cleopatra* from the sort of green kid in *Julius Caesar* to somebody who destroys Antony and Cleopatra and who seems to have no human feelings whatsoever. So that I think the paradox of the plays is that you spend all that time worrying is Julius Caesar any good, and you kill Julius Caesar, and what comes about is actually a worse political animal, which is Octavius; because I think that Octavius is finally much worse than Caesar. I mean, he has no humanity — it's shown in the galley scene, he has none at all. At least Julius Caesar was full of weakness and foible. No one likes Octavius in the plays, and I suspect neither does Shakespeare. But that doesn't answer your question?

RB Actually it does, because I think you're saying that part of the meaning of a Shakespeare play lies in other Shakespeare plays, which I think is profoundly true, and that the problems of *Julius Caesar* are only partially resolved by the end of that play. They are further illuminated by the *fact* of *Antony and Cleopatra* and I think that most people, if they had to choose between Octavius and Caesar would choose Caesar — I know I would — on the grounds that he is at least a human being if a badly flawed one, with human relationships. Whereas Octavius has no real human relationships (if we except his nominal counterpart, Octavia); he's simply a machine.

MK And I must also say that I was very involved in the idea of assassination. This is the country of assassins, and so assassination as a political act was very important for me to investigate in that play. You see, where it leaves you is, do you go out and bomb Hitler, do you kill Richard Nixon? It seems perfectly sensible to say yes, you do go out and kill Adolf Hitler, but you don't kill Richard Nixon; and yet again, is Richard Nixon responsible for the killing of I don't know how many people in the Vietnamese war? So violence as a political act concerned me, and I continually faced my ambivalences about it. And I thought, so did Shakespeare. I don't think I was just presenting my own confusion as Shakespeare's; I thought, it's there. It seems perfectly clear that Caesar needs to be eliminated from the state, and yet it also seems to be clear — I think that's why people don't like the second half of *Julius Caesar* — that it does present a sort of dissolution after the assassination. I think there is an implied criticism, or certainly a real investigation of what does an act of violence do to society? Does it save it? And the answer is clearly no. It may be necessary, but it doesn't save it. It changes it, but it doesn't solve the problem. And so it seemed to me to be false to create a Caesar who was just clearly Adolf Hitler. I mean there have been productions where Caesar was clearly Hitler or Mussolini. And I felt that that was simplifying the problem. Because we all know, yes, let's get rid of Adolf Hitler, and seven million people might have been alive today. But to see Caesar as Hitler and Brutus as a liberal is simplifying that play, and making the audience much more satisfied because they know exactly whose side to be on, who to be sympathetic with, and therefore to feel sorry for Brutus at the end. Brutus does behave quite badly much of the time.

RB It is, of course, possible for a production to detach itself equally from a proto-Fascist Caesar and a liberal Brutus.

MK To detach itself: what do you mean by that?

RB To invite no sympathy.

MK Yes, of course — I suppose you feel the same about liberals and proto-Fascists that I do! Yes, I guess what I'm really saying is that I'm struggling at the moment, really struggling with the fact that I am no longer sure that the director's job in Shakespeare is to interpret it.

I'm terribly aware that all my productions interpret Shakespeare in some way, but I don't think that finally it's what I wish to explore, because I think that an interpretation given to Shakespeare reduces Shakespeare; and what is extraordinary about Shakespeare is that he is in a sense irreducible, that it is bigger and beyond. As you said last night, it is the greatest intelligence that one comes across. And to interpret that is to make it smaller somehow, to make it less rich, less resonant. I am struggling now with a way of organising a production, because obviously you have to go into a rehearsal, and you do a production, and you do work with actors, and you do open it. And it is finally a piece. But the problem is still not to deny, not to give up that extraordinary richness that you get in no other playwright in the world. It really is the problem that concerns me the most and I have absolutely no answer to it except at the moment to give up things that I used to do, to give up saying 'this is an anti-war play,' or 'this is a play about such and such a thing.' I feel that of course interpretation always comes in, because these are areas of any given play of Shakespeare's, as we said to start with, that relate to the reasons for choosing that play for production. And if you choose a play of Shakespeare's you are immediately making an interpretation. And then my struggle is to fight against making it just about that. Of course, I didn't like Julius Caesar as a character, when I read *Julius Caesar*, and of course I was somewhat more sympathetic to Brutus. And then I had to fight against swinging the play in that direction, because I don't think that Shakespeare has. I think that Shakespeare is infinitely more interesting than I am! As a person I see two sides of every issue, which sometimes leads to inaction, though I don't think I am Hamlet, but it does lead to a pause in my thinking or action. And I think that is true of Shakespeare, but he sees three or four sometimes. And I would like that to be true in the audience. I did a production of *Henry V*, and I said to myself, what it was not was a pro-nationalist production. I thought it was trying to investigate what nationalism was, that it had its strengths and weaknesses, and that it did this, but it also did that; and people then went away saying this was an anti-war production. I don't think I specifically sat down to think of giving this impression. I might have. But now I would hope that if somebody went to see a production of mine, and said this is an anti-war production — I would hope that that was what they got out of it, not what I necessarily was saying.

    RB Yes, I sympathise very much with this account of the director's problem. Obviously, the director can never leave the duty of interpretation. Everything he does in his relations with the actors, say, is a series of decisions and the decisions must presumably be related, if only tangentially, to a central judgement. On the other hand, I can see that an overly thematic production, a production which too rigidly insists on negating certain possibilities in the text, is a way of approach that you feel has nothing for you now.

MK Yes, very little for me now. I think that at the moment I am really endeavouring to make the opposites in Shakespeare exist equally, or simultaneously, and it's very difficult to bring an audience along with you that way, because audiences so much want to be told what to think. One of the reasons, I'm afraid, that people have been going to Shakespeare for a long time is because in a sense they thought he would tell them what to think. And then they feel so insecure when they are not. When I went to school we were told that that was indeed what Shakespeare did. I mean, I think I was taught that Shakespeare was a moralist (something I absolutely don't believe in at all any more), that he had a firm sense of moral order, and that one could go to Shakespeare to celebrate order. Well, there may be harmony or resolution in Shakespeare, but I'm not sure that it's order in the sense that I was originally brought to believe. And I think audiences still go to Shakespeare because they know who's good and who's bad, and who to be sympathetic with; and I think that's not Shakespearian. And so I'm endeavouring to change them around! With the material by a writer that has become in the cultural pantheon a representative, in an odd way, of the *status quo*. And yet of course he is really revolutionary at the same time. That sets up a wonderful tension, and it's all those tensions that interest me. To get the audience to come along with you, to feel that they're on an uncharted voyage, is what I would really like followers of Shakespeare to be, and I would like the audience to come in without their passports and without their maps; and think perhaps that if they crossed the sea they might fall off in the end, or they might possibly get to India. You know, I would like that sense of daring, and very often one goes to terrible excesses in order to do that, which I've certainly been guilty of, but that is the method.

RB But the audience needs some bearings, doesn't it?

MK I'd like to give them *two*. I'd like to give them in one scene, one, and then I'd like to change it in the other which is what I think is in the play, and then I'd like them to resolve that. Perhaps when they go home. I'd like it not to be so linear.

RB Perhaps we could think of this in terms of presentation of character, of the problems of psychology, which one has to arrive at with any character. Shylock, for instance, is clearly different in several major scenes.

MK A score of characters are like that. Shylock is, certainly, and Portia is too — the two major characters are.

RB So how do you approach this problem, that people appear to *be* somewhat different identities in different scenes?

MK This is a central question at the moment, because both actors and audiences have been trained to believe in a unified conception of characters, to look for that, and when they don't see it to think something's wrong. Audiences think something's wrong — either the actor is not acting well or the play is not well written if they cannot pinpoint the essence of a character through unified behaviour. That is also true of our actors — especially in America — who are brought up to understand characterisation as behaviour in a certain way. Modern psychology allows us to realise that the self is really a series of identities. When I left my analysis — I must tell you this, that I left my analysis after four or five years, when I realised that the questions that were being asked of me by my analyst were, are you a Jew, are you a Christian, are you this, are you that? And I said those were not questions that concerned me, and I realised that in Freudian analysis those were important questions, and I was unintegrated if I could not make those categorisations. I left my analyst. I felt that we were now getting into areas that I disagreed with, and I was not going to pursue that. And I understand much better from people like Norman Brown, Herbert Marcuse, and R. D. Laing, that that is an irrelevant question. I think that's true of characterisation in Shakespeare.

And so, to get back to your question about Shylock, I no longer try to figure out why Shylock is behaving *against* his characterisation, when he behaves differently in one scene from another. I begin to go from the other way, and say, all of those are Shylock. You see, I used to say, Shylock is such-and-such, and when he behaves nicely or when he behaves meanly, it is uncharacteristic of him, and therefore the other actor must be something to make him behave uncharacteristically, or, he must have a hidden motive, or he must — as we say in acting jargon — 'take a character adjustment' at that moment. Because his 'real' character exists in, let's say, the scene with Jessica. This is hypothetical, I do not believe this, but I've worked with a Shylock who did. He felt that the 'real' Shylock comes out in the scene with Jessica, when he's a good father, who really wants to protect his daughter, and who is basically a generous man who is forced by circumstances to become a usurer, etc., etc. And so, when he is met on the Rialto, and makes the suggestion about the pound of flesh – I've worked with a prominent and extremely able actor, who found a way that the pound of flesh was actually, at that time, a joke! And I think that's poppycock. I think that you don't say now, this is the scene where the real Shylock emerges, and the other scenes are Shylock reacting to outer circumstances. I now prefer to say, no: these are contradictions in the character, and the contradictions make up the character. That is, oddly enough, the hardest thing to get across to anyone. It is almost impossible to get that across to actors, because they feel adrift, for they too have been conditioned to say, 'I must find the line, the through line, for the character.' It is almost impossible to get it across to audiences, because audiences don't like to feel that. They like to be able to say, 'so-and-so is such-and-such.' And I know it doesn't seem like a difficult process, but I promise you, it's the hardest.

RB This may well be one of the ways of defining Shakespearian drama. What I think you get in almost all other drama is this: either there is a clear-cut through line for the actors to grasp, or there are certain disparities and contradictions in the behaviour of the characters which we suspect we can relate to the exigencies of playwriting, and perhaps, in a more-or-less disguised way, to the incompetence of the playwright. Whereas we still feel that the contradictions and paradoxes of behaviour in Shakespearian drama can none the less be related to a central self.

MK I think you must make a decision. Either you think that Shakespeare had a wonderful mind but was a dreadful playwright, or you decide that he had a wonderful mind but was a great playwright! If you think he was a great playwright, which I do, then you do not say to yourself, because this does not seem to make logical sense it's bad playwriting. I think you say no, then why is that then? That he is aware of what we are aware of now: that I talk to you now, and that I go and talk to my students, and then I go and talk to my teacher, and then I go and talk to someone that I'm in love with, and that you all meet together in a room and talk without mentioning my name, and you can come up with four different people. They are all me. And that is true about Shakespearian characters. When you asked me what one brings to another kind of play from Shakespeare – well, what I bring to Ibsen now is that I search for and relish contradictions in characters in well-made plays. And try to emphasise them, because I find that to be much truer than to say, this is the given for that character. You see, it's very easy for me to interpret a play; it's the simplest thing for me to do, to say that this play is about this. I have been brought up that way. I went to school that way, and wrote book reports about the author's point of view. I was taught to find out the spine of a play and the theme of a play, and interpretation is something that comes reasonably simple to me. And I have just come to the conclusion — I don't want to quote Susan Sontag, but I am becoming *against* interpretation, and I am continually fighting my desire to tie things up, and to categorise and to interpret. And I must also say that of course as a director, the minute you interpret a play everybody talks about your direction. They like it or they don't like it, but they sure as hell talk about you as a director. It's 'Michael Kahn's production of . . .', because all you have to do is to have a sort of concept they talk about. Part of the fun of it for me was doing that, and I'm in the process of trying to free myself from that. Let's say that's where I'm about at the moment.

    RB Let's consider one or two of the technical implications of this. How about period analogies?

    MK Well, I'll tell you: I don't really believe in period analogies. I would prefer to do everything in the period it was written in, I would prefer to do everything in Elizabethan or Renaissance, and avoid making another reference, or inference through metaphors. I have done almost all my productions in Elizabethan dress or in modern dress, and I have always been able to justify in my mind modern dress, because I keep saying to myself, well, doublets and hose were all modern dress anyway, when they put on a funny little thing over doublet and hose in *Julius Caesar* that really was modern dress. So it's all right to do things in modern dress, because somehow that kind of tension probably existed during Shakespeare's time. I don't really approve of taking another historical period. However, I'm about to do that with a play for the very first time in my life, with *Romeo and Juliet*. And this is only because I have an enormous feeling that the film has really investigated the visual aspects of the Renaissance so completely that there's no way for us to do it; so I just said I must think of it differently, I'm going to set it in another period. It's an English play, but Italy is always Italy. I looked for a period in which there would be a reason for a vendetta, and I looked for a period in which there would be a genuine generation gap. I found this just after the Risorgimento, when families just didn't speak to each other. There was a *nouveau riche* aristocracy, that was on the side of the House of Savoy, and the Papal aristocracy was conservative and out of fashion and so it seemed to fit in some kind of way. At least it frees me from feeling that I'm continually stuck, with everything reminding me of the Zeffirelli production and feeling the need to be different. You see, I've seen the

Zeffirelli production twice and I saw the movie, and one of the dangers I'm now beginning to avoid is trying to see wonderful productions of Shakespeare. Nothing in the world could get me to do *A Midsummer Night's Dream* now. After I saw Peter Hall's production of *Twelfth Night* ten years ago, nothing could have gotten me to do *Twelfth Night*. When one sees a production that one feels at that moment is definitive — it doesn't change year by year, you know, so it takes a long while for something to be not definitive any longer. Zeffirelli's is the definitive Renaissance version of a play I find less interesting than many others, anyway. I don't think I'll ever see a definitive *King Lear*, thank God, nor will I do one, so therefore one can continually go to see *Lears*. But *Romeo and Juliet*, which I think is not nearly so rich as many of the other plays, is more obvious in many ways, much more simple and not about anything other than it's about, Zeffirelli really did, for me. Maybe ten years from now I'll think differently, but I've found that I have to do *Romeo and Juliet* this year for those administrative reasons we mentioned earlier, so I've just had to get myself together, and I've decided to set it in the nineteenth century, and so it will at least give me a back-door way of coming to the play. Also it will not make me feel that I have to be different or clever. If I did a Renaissance version I would be feeling how can I do that differently? I hate it when directors feel they have to be clever. I would probably find myself always saying, 'Now how can I do that in another way?' and I don't want to deal with that, because I don't think that's very artistic. So I've put it in the nineteenth century, and I know therefore that people can read newspapers and smoke cigars and have sewing-machines; and I know the Nurse can now be at the sewing-machine during the speech when she says 'she stinted and said "aye" ' instead of fanning herself as she does in every other production, and so that at least is a way of getting to it. Of course people will think it's a concept, and really it isn't, it's just *décor*, but there you are!

   RB Of course, it's not pejorative to call a concept 'decorative', it's simply a way of categorising it.

   MK Many people do take a look at *décor*, and think that's a concept; that's one of the reasons for getting rid of *décor*. I think those theatres such as Stratford, Ontario, that in a sense have no *décor* are perhaps more able to get to the heart of a play than those theatres that, for each play, must come up with, 'What will this look like?' And you know, very often that time in rehearsal, when we're just in the rehearsal room with jeans or whatever it is we have on, is truer than when all of a sudden the fanciness comes in later on. And I think Peter

Brook must have found that out, because while everyone talked on and on about the *décor* of the *Dream* — I've not asked Peter Brook about this, but it looked to me like a rehearsal room that I rehearse in, it looked like a white studio. It didn't look like an idea for *A Midsummer Night's Dream*, it looked like a place in which you would rehearse a production of *A Midsummer Night's Dream*. And all those wonderful props very much looked like rehearsal props. We cannot use the real props because of union regulations — it looked like they went out and bought those things in day-glo colours, and I suspect that that wonderful Sally Jacobs set is based on a room they rehearsed in, not an idea for the *Dream*. I have had that experience when a play has been truer to me in rehearsal when we have not had *décor*, and have seen something else happen that has been not as good when the *décor* is on.

RB But do you think there's a serious case to be made when a production points to a real period, or a real historical analogy, and wishes the play to be interpreted through that analogy?

MK Well, I don't think you're going to learn more about *Coriolanus* by setting it in Napoleonic France. And to be honest, I don't think we're going to learn more about *Romeo and Juliet* by setting it in the Risorgimento, even though anyone who does know the Risorgimento might perhaps understand the feud. But I have seen a Napoleonic *Coriolanus*, and to think of Coriolanus as Napoleon makes the play less interesting. I don't see what you get from it. It is easier for some people in the audience to assimilate, because they know more about Napoleon than Coriolanus. But it doesn't tell you a thing. It may tell you more about Napoleon, but it doesn't tell you any more about Coriolanus — it actually tells you less about Coriolanus. If you want to do a play about Napoleon, then maybe it's a good idea to do *Coriolanus*! But if you want to do *Coriolanus* then it's not a production to make at all.

RB I confess I rather agree with this, certainly with your instance, but for the purposes of argument let me push it a little further. Suppose we say that Shakespeare — what we call 'Shakespeare' — is ultimately intelligence, and 'Shakespeare' for us is cognition, we know more all the time because history is evolving and we with it: why may we not allude to the more that we know?

MK I think any artist who's working does that. I don't think there's any way of not doing that. I think when you simply pick up the text and start to work on it, then your work is the sum of your experience. I don't know how you deny that. What you're asking me is how does one *physicalise* that? Now I think that that is unnecessary. It doesn't

offend me when I see it, but I think that it has a tendency to change
the issue. I don't see how any artist working does not bring to bear
everything that he knows or perceives. The wonderful thing about
Shakespeare is that he adds to your perception, in the same way
that history does. I keep suspecting that although one says that the
reason that audiences go to Shakespeare is because they love the
poetry, or they love the pageantry, they really go because it actually
does change perception. And if art has any function (and function is a
word I recoil from) it is to change or increase perception. I think that's
what Shakespeare does, and I don't think it's necessary, say, to set it
in 2001 or an historical period to do that. One's sensitivity to situation,
to character, to relationships, to all of that, comes out of one's awareness and does not need to be concretised by information about the
French Revolution, or about the Industrial Revolution, or about the
1930s. The *Julius Caesar* of Orson Welles is a famous production, but
Julius Caesar is not about Mussolini. And that's all you see, a play
about Mussolini. And actually the issue about Mussolini is probably
easier to do than the issue about Julius Caeser.

RB You've been arguing all the time against a reductionist Shakespeare, against a reduced Shakespeare. How do you relate this strategy
to the frontal difficulty of the text, and cutting the text, especially?

MK I'm cutting less and less and less. I'm terribly aware that
when you cut Shakespeare, you immediately edit out the things you
don't think fit, and so you're immediately doing exactly what I disagree
with. As a matter of fact, I'm going into rehearsals without edited
script, and the editing now — I hope my actors will forgive me —is
very often to do with our inadequacies rather than Shakespeare's. I
don't edit very much any more. I edited those musicians out of *Romeo
and Juliet* partly for economic reasons. I'm perverse enough to think,
wouldn't it be fun to do it, but it is also an Elizabethan joke, and I
must confess I find Elizabethan jokes less amusing. And so when they
are really Elizabethan puns, I cannot really feel that anyone will care
when I let them go. It's a great deal of money less on salaries, three
fewer costumes, and also four minutes that the audience isn't going
to understand anyway because they don't have any clues about Simon
Catling and 'heart's ease' and all that. But I am editing less, and that's
because I am merely enjoying more things that don't fit in with the
things before. And so we're getting longer and longer productions in
Connecticut! But then you know I would no more dream of cutting out
something from *Tristan and Isolde*. I even think there's something
about Shakespeare, that even if you are bored, once you pass the

boredom you come into some sort of ecstatic region; it's wonderful. It's like Buddhism, you arrive at a changing of your time, the organisation of your rhythm – Shakespeare demands that of you. You come in with the rhythm that you had all day long, busying yourself in your office, a twentieth-century rhythm, and he asks you to change that rhythm. And that's very hard, you know; audiences want a play to match their particular kind of hurry and quickness, and I think you can fight that. And if you change your rhythm, you change your sense of time, and you come out with something else. That's why I begin to like all those impossible, in modern terms, ordering of Shakespeare's plays where you see one set of characters in the first scene, and another set of characters in the second scene, then a third set of characters in the third scene; and the plot, *per se*, doesn't really get started till about the fifth scene. And of course you could cut, bang-bang-snap, into the situation, but those sorts of scenes have, I find, that ability to make the audience say OK, I don't expect this to go like a television show, I don't expect this to go the way my day at the office has been, I must succumb to this in some way. And I think that when you do you find the richness is there, and you notice things you wouldn't notice otherwise.

    RB In the necessary compromises that one makes between the plays and the audience, then, you I think are drawing the line more and more towards the play.

    MK Yes, I think I always did, but I think that I brought something else – my 'ideas' about the play!

    RB How do you approach the problems, for instance, of verse speaking? How do you mediate between the text and your audience in that way?

    MK Well, as an American, we have less of a tradition of a certain kind of verse speaking. We have not really heard very much verse speaking in that particular kind of way that wasn't poor and artificial. So at the moment part of my concern as a director is to actually get my actors to enjoy verse, and to see it as the vehicle and the tool with which to deal. I'm still trying to get there with my actors and myself. Most American actors believe in a kind of emotional truth to plays, and very often in some cases it is at the expense of the verse, or the verse is at the expense of the emotional truth. And right now, at this point in my life, and in the company's life, I'm trying to find how to put these two together. But that is really my concern with words now, it doesn't really have very much to do with the audience, it has to do with our handling of it. Because we still sometimes are a little funny about that, we sometimes feel that when we speak verse we must do it as a purely technical thing; if we are also going to feel, we drop the verse. And I believe that both must happen. That is what I think eventually American Shakespeare will be. That is what I'm trying to find, and so that is my concern — how to get us, that is the company and myself, to really enjoy, savour, use the verse and not feel it apart from the situation, in the life of the character. And that is a serious consideration now. And I think if I can find the answer, then I can truly call us the American Shakespeare Theater. Of course, people ask us all the time, what does American Shakespeare mean? It must mean something other than doing Shakespeare in America. I teach at Juillard, and I think my involvement there is how to mix technical facility with that specifically American desire to arrive at emotional truth. And I think that one can say that there's a difference between American acting and, let's say, British or Canadian acting. Great actors are great actors; they can somehow manage to do both. But there's a suspicion of words in America, and there's an over-reliance on words in much of British acting, and I would like to bring the two together in the American Shakespeare Theater.

RB So what, ultimately, is Shakespeare for you?

MK It's the best play, the best playwright that one can ever deal with, and for me it is the best way to investigate everything that one knows, and find out more.

ROBIN PHILLIPS

Ralph Berry You are the Artistic Director of the Stratford Shakespearean Festival Foundation of Canada. How much does this word
'Shakespearean' commit you to Shakespeare, in any season?

Robin Phillips We are, unquestionably, predominantly a Shakespeare
festival. We have a charter for our Foundation that stresses that we
shall promote the knowledge of, the awareness of, Shakespeare; and
the cultural and theatrical growth in Canada through Shakespearean
and other works, but predominantly through Shakespeare. I'm not sure
that I agree with 'Shakespeare Festivals', or indeed with Festivals
related to any specific author. But nevertheless that's what we are. Why
don't I agree with it? The problem of having to come up with a season
of Shakespeare plays is remarkably difficult. If you're not careful
you're left with a merry-go-round choice and the plays just happen to
come round again because it's now six years since they were last done.
And that's no reason for re-doing it. It's possible that when a play
comes round again it's the right time, but the biggest problem I have
is choosing plays that seem to be right for the time.

There are many factors that make a play right for its time, not just
to do with Shakespeare, but with what theatre is there for. You have
first to know why you're in the theatre, what theatre is supposed to be
offering; if it's there in some way to illuminate people's lives, to
stimulate thought, progress, whatever it may be. Then, the choice of
plays in one sense is limited. I'm fortunate in my festival that it
happens to be Shakespeare. There can be no other author who has
covered more widely the whole range of human behaviour. One is pretty
likely to find a play that will work for each year. I think to find a
season of plays that will work for each year is pretty unlikely, and you
are bound to have to choose some plays that are just being done again,
and you hope the entertainment value will be enough to justify its
choice. But at least one play a season will have something specific to
say to that audience that year.

RB You've just had a very successful season, both critically and in
the popular esteem. Going entirely on the reviews, one would perhaps
suggest that your most successful production has been *Measure for
Measure*. Perhaps you would agree with this? And could you tell us
why? What is there in this play, and your production especially, which

91

has got across, here and now, to the audience that you encounter?

RP   First of all, we have to admit that we're fortunate in having a play that isn't seen all that often. That's a help. It's also a play that possibly has been out of favour for a while, or not seemed important enough to warrant a revival. It is possible to explore the essential sexual core of the play now. Clearly there have been periods since it was written when this would not have been possible. And here we are at the time when people are prepared to accept it; a play that pivots on that central theme is permissible in 1975, for a start. I think also that the other themes of power, corruption in power, sexual blackmail in power, are interesting. I suppose a thousand plays can relate in some sense to Watergate; but corruption, whether or not Watergate had any sexual motives at its core, is neither here nor there. The fact that we've had a major scandal at that level allows one to explore a play with that as plot. And consequently one is prepared to delve into the reasons — not the ones that we've explored in our newspapers, but totally differ-ent. I also think of all Shakespeare's plays, it's the most ambiguous. He leaves so many questions unanswered. And one senses that ambiguity is something that is allowed; we are prepared to accept more, theatrically, in unanswered questions, and to answer them for ourselves. This play is not resolved, and I think we can find excitement and theatricality in its lack of resolution.

Measure for Measure is also a very strong play for the misuse, or the rights of, women. By that I don't mean that I think it's a Women's Lib play. But there are questions posed that suggest these problems, that are very much on our minds. It's International Women's Year, the year we do our play. And certainly the central female figure has many of those questions posed but not answered, centuries before they're being asked again — questions in the forefront of our minds, the front pages of our newspapers. There aren't many Shakespeare plays that have that. Then there's the re-questioning in the play of who's right, who's wrong. It's a good time to say to oneself, but the man is called Angelo, and presumably Shakespeare knew what he was doing when he called him that. Lucio (Light) perhaps isn't just low-life, therefore to do with corruption and degrading qualities, but perhaps is able from that sort of background to produce truth. I think we're prepared to accept now that honesty and nobility don't necessarily spring from the upper classes but can be found in the lower orders. In previous productions and writings on the play the Duke, because he's the Head of State, has appeared the one who must be in the right. Perhaps we're prepared to change the structure now, and say that maybe it's the one at the top

who's in error. The man at the bottom may be the one with the seed
of humanity, the seed of truth. And somewhere in between people get
trapped. I think the times are right for that revaluation.

RB I take your central points about the sexuality and the ambiguity
of *Measure for Measure*, and I think it's absolutely so that they
correspond to profound movements of our times, especially with
regard to the questions raised concerning the position of women.
And also the questions concerning the whole authority-subordinate
relationship. On both these issues we're inclined to view things very
differently from even a few years ago, let alone a generation ago, and
this must modify considerably any production of *Measure for Measure*
today. Could we think more specifically of the metaphoric vehicle
for your production? I'm thinking of the fact that you locate it in the
Vienna of 1912. Now what considerations guided you to that year?

RP Basically, a sense of repression, and that could have taken one
into a reasonable range of Victorian/early Edwardian periods. Things
hinted at but not talked about — things pious outside, but a sense of
stronger sexuality produced by the fact that it isn't talked about.
The specific period came about because of *Duke* and because of *Vienna*,
and trying to find a period when Duke as Head of State could fit quite
easily into one's mind without one saying, 'But shouldn't he be a King,
or Prime Minister, or whatever?' Just the acceptance that that title
and Head of State could go together. There's also, I guess, a
fascination with the fact that Isabella seems to me struggling to become
a nun; she's none too sure that the order she's entering is going to be
strict enough. I was fascinated by an order founded by (I can't
remember her name) about this time, where the nun's habits were
made by the equivalent of a Dior, and it was a select little group that
she got together. They lived with their own code of behaviour and
beliefs, but nevertheless they had the extravagance of Worth stitching
up their habits.

Clearly the play has venereal disease problems lurking as a
foundation for the sexual repression. It was necessary to look for a
period that contains that too, matching the period that Shakespeare
wrote for. I don't, strangely enough, find the play Elizabethan. There
are some plays that I do strongly see as Elizabethan. Certainly at the
moment, the only way in which they should be presented is as
Elizabethan. I don't feel that with this piece. It's very hard to tell:
there's something about the tightness of the language, the imagery;
it isn't as abundant, as rich as in many of the plays. It's tighter in its
phraseology. Shakespeare of course is nearly always precise, but not in

the same unrelenting vein that this play has, and that I think was
going towards the military, the high dresses that went from the neck
to the ankle with nothing showing.

RB Could you elaborate on some of the costuming for the main
characters which embodied your concept?

RP Well, first of all it was bureaucracy. Everything to do with the
Duke and Angelo was frock-coated, stiff, starched, pristine collars and
cuffs, a sense of well-scrubbed fingernails. We actually saw Angelo's
desk being polished by a bevy of servants, every detail of it gleaming,
no dust, no filth. No naked light, for instance, but flames and oil-
lamps surrounded by smoky domes — the fact that it's *naked* is
immediately not permissible. Isabella's dress, following through the
order that is in the script, basically a white-dressed order, was made
in an incredibly soft jersey, so that although she was buttoned from
neck to ankle the movement of the material constantly showed the
female form beneath. That's another thing that drives me to
another period for the play. There was a time when it was a boy
playing the part, so that the body could not be part of the performance in one sense. Now we have actresses who can do things with their
bodies. Part of the interpretation is how the body moves, how the body
responds. And I think that to ignore the fact that we now have the
enormous advantage of the female body playing a female role is to
ignore our time. The awareness of breasts, however beautifully
covered — there is no mistaking that it's the genuine article, and not a
fourteen-year-old boy padded up to play the role. A sense constantly
of military very close to the high-ranking officials — Prime Minister,
leader, Duke, Head of State, whatever it may be. Also a strange
relationship between the Duke and Friar Peter, whereby one assumes
from the brief snatch of conversation that is picked up midway that
the Friar has assumed he's come there for some reason of the heart,
and it's OK for him to come for that motive, although the Duke
quickly tells him why he's come there. I think it's important to smell
Vienna. I've seen the play many times when I've enjoyed the society,
but it could have been set anywhere: *Vienna* is important. The
specifics of the locations where Shakespeare sets his plays are always
remarkably accurate.

RB Can I question you about that, since I'm not quite sure what
you mean. It's obvious that to us Vienna is, let's say, still the capital
of the Austro-Hungarian Empire. We associate with it a certain
gemütlich style of life, a certain array of good things to eat, a certain
atmosphere and gaiety of the entire community, and so on. I agree

about the specifics of a Shakespeare setting, but I wonder if
Shakespeare's Vienna has any kind of connection with what we think
of as Vienna? Isn't Shakespeare's 'Vienna' a code-word for a society,
which he has imagined in every detail, but which cannot be illustrated
from our knowledge of the place called 'Vienna' by us?

RP I think you're absolutely right that his Vienna doesn't have
to be the 'Vienna' as we know it today. Nevertheless Shakespeare
does establish very clearly, whether it's by some strange prophetic
talent, a low-life gaiety and freedom that isn't far from, or doesn't
take much imagination to see it fitting into the Vienna that we know
about; together with an extremely sophisticated, knowledgeable,
principled upper stratum. I think the interesting one is the political
position of the state. That is essential, it's the big one in a strangely
positioned group of principalities. It isn't a major power – the
Duke would be busier, one feels, if it were! Shakespeare's set it
where it isn't a major power, therefore there is time for more
intrigue, for a principal of state to take time off and become a friar
and just lurk around his country. One can't envisage that in the
America of today. I could envisage it possibly in a Switzerland of
today, a smaller pivotal state but not a major power. There's also
the question of time and where he's going and how long he's going
to be away, those sorts of things, which geographically make
reasonable sense.

It can't be by accident that somewhere around that part of Europe
we eventually find Freud. I'm not sure that I can accept that Freud
might have happened in Italy. There's a national climate that produces
varying forms of greatness. In this extraordinary play there's a quality
that one senses, however many centuries before that it was written,
that seems to be absolutely right for the place. I would not be
surprised to find that Freud or Ibsen were devoted to *Measure for
Measure*. I do think that the play has such remarkable silent motivating
forces that it could have stimulated those minds.

RB I think you've certainly laid your finger, with Freud, on a
permanent reality of the play, even though it seems patently unhistori-
cal to say so. Vienna, obviously, is numerous cities. Vienna can stand
for us as Schnitzler's city – that clearly doesn't seem to resemble the
play very closely. But through a curious chance of history, Vienna is
also Freud's city. And that does indeed seem to describe the play that
we know very well, precisely because the play is concerned to such an
incredible extent with repressed sexuality. Here, one feels, it's possible
to pick up the chance of history, to identify a particular Vienna that

we — I mean a general cultivated audience — would know, and at the same time say that this Vienna, Freud's Vienna, is an admirable and perhaps ideal physical embodiment of the city Shakespeare described.

RP I absolutely agree with all that. I don't, though, plan productions with the most elaborate, calculating intellectual response. I start with my own basic knowledge, and intuition is the first thing that happens. I think it's impossible to remove oneself in that play. Once you start with repressed sexuality, you are bound to think of Freud now, we can't ignore the fact that we know about him. Once that happens, the visual side of the play leaps at you constantly. It's also extra-ordinary that there are very few references (unlike the other plays) to Elizabethan dress. There's one reference to 'cod-piece' which can either be simply removed, or left in. We do still talk about cod-pieces, we do know about them! There's no reason why 'cod-piece' shouldn't be mentioned in a modern play. It could just as easily be set in Berlin, at a certain time. One senses something slightly looser. For a time I toyed with Berlin, in the thirties, and the possibility that productions like *Cabaret* have given us an insight into the seamy side of life that could work for the low-life of the play. But there's an authoritarian element there that's stronger than the actual text suggests. It is strict, but delicate; it has a fineness, a texture. For instance, you go to the architecture of Vienna in 1912. It has for me a quality that exactly matches the strictness but delicacy of texture of the play's language. That is important, not only what people wear but what they live in. 'Moated grange' is Elizabethan/Jacobean, of course, but also there's a smell of romance hidden in the term. It's the idea of cut-off, repressed, again; but it's the combination of a period that allows you to smell romance, gaiety ('her reputation was disvalued in levity') plus strictness and repression that finally narrows you down until you arrive at where you think it exactly matches the Vienna-structure of the play.

RB I'm fascinated by the untaken possibilities that you've been talking about. I can see very well, for instance, that Isherwood's Berlin would go half the way towards *Measure for Measure*, but not the other half. I don't see how Isabella and Angelo could possibly fit in (for most of us) into Isherwood's Berlin, though Pompey and Mistress Overdone would so so superbly. Part of the problem is what people know. For instance, if one were to set *Measure for Measure* in the Renaissance, rather late, and put it into what appears the Restoration: now, what most of us know about the Restoration, rightly or wrongly, is that repression was a non-starter. This may be a

total historical solecism; for all we know, people by and large were as
repressed in 1670 as 1912. But that is not what we think we know.
Consequently, a late-Renaissance production of *Measure for Measure*
would fail, because of our knowledge. At least, it would fail if it set
out to keep strongly in mind the idea of sexual repression. And we can
hardly avoid that.

RP Right. We're hardly likely to find posters telling you how you
can find treatment for VD in the period we chose, although it is quite
clear from the text that it was very much there. It's treated as a
scandalous joke, but not nearly with the abandonment that it's treated
in the Restoration. I was struck by someone who said, 'but capital
punishment for the crime of getting a woman pregnant' — you have
first of all to accept that that couldn't happen in 1912. Once you've
accepted that, the period works very well. It is amazing to me that as
recently as Queen Victoria, a law banning the practice of homosexual
acts *for men* was brought in, and when it was repealed recently it was
discovered to most people's amazement (to mine, certainly) that
there wasn't one for females, because Victoria would not accept that
such a thing could happen. It seems to me that if that could be the
case in Victorian times, it is just as easy to believe that somebody could
say, 'And you will be put to death for such an act.' Nobody apparently
waged any great battle to convince the Queen that such acts were
possible. Because she was so horrified and said that nobody could do
such a thing, it was dropped, and there was no law.

RB I must say I've long imagined *Measure for Measure* as being
essentially a Victorian play, and I imagine a sub-title 'The Other
Viennese' for my ideal production. The only other period and society
that I know at all, that seems to be compatible with the text of the
play, is that of New England in the early seventeenth century, with
those amazing statutes prohibiting adultery and related indiscretions
that remained on the books until very recently. I dare say that in some
cases they are still technically enforceable in Massachusetts and elsewhere in New England.

RP That's exactly the argument too for *Measure for Measure* in
1912. It's clear that nobody in the play believes that the law is *right*
— it's something that's been left on the statutes and just been
forgotten. Nobody in the play takes it seriously, they all say it's
scandalous, and the criticism levelled at the 1912 setting (that we
cannot believe this law stood then) is to assume that it was accepted
as it stood. The whole point is that the play says that it's monstrous
and that it shouldn't stand. In the same way it's taken us until a few

years ago to remove Victoria's feelings about homosexuality. It's an absurd law and just as silly, but it takes a great deal of time to get it removed.

RB The play actually identifies the absurdity very subtly. It does so by concentrating on the point that what is evil about the sexual act is that it results in pregnancy. Thus we have the pregnant Juliet who is paraded as an emblem of sin and shame, and is obliged to endure a sermon by the Duke. Thus also we have Isabella who at one point says very significantly to the Duke, 'I had rather my brother die by the law than my son should be unlawfully born.' So in this play morality tends to be defined pragmatically, by its fruits.

RP There's a clear difference too in the treatment of a bawd or a pimp, where presumably there is a reasonable amount of skill going into the act to prevent it from bearing fruit. They're treated in an entirely different way from the ones who actually go through with the whole thing with love, with consideration, but unlawfully bringing forth children. But I think the behaviour to the low-life — to the bawds, pimps and brothels — is entirely different, it's not considered as bad.

RB If I've understood your position correctly, then, you are eclectic on the whole question of costuming a Shakespeare play. You are prepared to set some plays in Renaissance (or mediaeval or Roman, presumably) if you believe it is appropriate for that play. Equally, you are prepared to seek your analogue from any period of history, if this seems right for the play.

RP The most important thing is to get through to the audience. Whatever thought you are trying to share has to happen spontaneously — it must be received with as much spontaneity as it is possible with our cumulative talents to achieve. If that means allowing the actress to use her body as an extra tool, which Shakespeare didn't have at his command, then that we should certainly use. If it's to allow an in-experienced company to first of all know themselves, and not to appear as masks or symbols but to be recognisable people with hearts, souls, hands and limbs, that is important. Hence using a modern dress approach for the first two productions of my young company here. I hope what they've discovered about themselves and how to stand on a stage and communicate directly with audiences they will now be able to take into a Renaissance period production, but still remain in contact with their modern audience. They won't suddenly assume a stance or a mask-type attitude to their character, but say 'I still have blood, skin, pores — I can sweat, I can bleed, I can suffer in the same way as the people that I am sharing with.'

I also think that there are some plays where we may not know the period at first hand — I don't know 1912 in that way — but 1912 is connected more directly with my life than centuries before. I've often seen newsreels of living people, I haven't just read it in books or seen paintings or pictures. Somewhere there is a connection that is more tangible. It's amazing how many people said to me that it was in modern dress, and I know exactly what they meant. They sensed that they were connected with a period that was to do with their lifetime. Not from history books, not from collections of objects, furniture, photographs, paintings, whatever it may be, but most have a relation, a grandmother or grandfather who was directly connected with the period. There is a much stronger link than if you go back a few centuries, and you can only piece together imaginatively all the documentation and arrive at what you hope it was. But the actuality is there and I think that produces a very special smell for an audience, it hits somewhere quite different.

Then there's the importance of the end of the play, of the dastardly behaviour of the Duke — the omnipotence, the lack of sensitivity towards any other human being, only his own thought, only what he wanted; this, happening in such a ruthless manner in a period where within a very short space of time one would be into a major war, seemed to be another essential quality. History now makes clear to us, I think, that strange things happened to people's morals in those lulls. God forbid that one should appear to be saying, 'We need wars' every so often, but if we could look at history and see how our morals decline or the sort of behaviour patterns that finally have produced major wars, we might be able to do something about it before they happen. There is a recurring theme.

RB I suspect that most of us have a deep sense that the most important event in the twentieth century is the 1914-18 war, and that the primary episodes that have entered modern consciousness are grouped around that event. To take up modernity from another angle, you were speaking earlier about *Two Gentlemen of Verona*, and the extent to which it helped your actors to know certain things about themselves. And this tied in with the fact that in your production you make it explicitly about four young people who are very immature, who are imperfectly aware of their identities. At the end of the play they are very obviously asking questions about themselves and their relationships, and are not at all resting upon any illusory security in the text as we receive it.

RP What I feel most about that play is the infuriating hint at
muscle that constantly comes up, the feeling that any moment we
might develop into *Twelfth Night* or *As You Like It* — but it never
does. The characters are just too young, they don't have the muscles,
the development, the competences, the total personality. But then one
has to say, 'You can't act that' unless it is part of the given circumstances. It is an unformed person, a person who doesn't yet know
himself. He hasn't developed his own muscles; it isn't just an author
who hasn't supplied them for him, it's a boy who hasn't yet
discovered about the world about him, about anybody else. One feels
that a lot of those characters could swap lines. They could just as
easily be placed in each other's mouth; they're that undisciplined. And
to come to the end of the play with any resolution is a mistake. The
play does not resolve, they have not found maturity by the end. Their
passions change from day to day, from minute to minute. To say by
the end of the play they have now found the first footing and will
continue is absurd. There is no suggestion, I think, that they will
develop along certain lines. What we tried to say at the end is, 'And
that's as far as it goes. But tomorrow we may well be looking in the
other direction. We still have not found ourselves.'

RB And all this marries up happily with the pool-side location in
Verona, which takes modernity in one direction about as far as it can
go. So far we've been talking, broadly, about the general and strategic
considerations that a director has to bear in mind. What about the
tactical, and perhaps unplannable situations? Do you find that in
rehearsals certain scenes emerge, certain facts of the first order emerge,
which you haven't strictly speaking planned, but have set in motion?

RP Yes. Basically, of course, it's understood that what we are
trying to do is to get to the core of the text, to find out what the guy
was trying to say, what the motivations were for the characters, what
he wanted to share with his audience. To get to the heart of that
matter requires trust to go into any territory that may prove fruitful.
It may prove otherwise, but there has to be a trust between actor and
director that any territory is worth delving into, to see if it produces an
essential core that might be hidden.

We had quite an interesting one in the Ophelia mad scenes recently.
I've a dread of those pixie Ophelias who rush around with wild
flowers looking fey and pathetic, clutching at slightly disarrayed hair,
and I'm slightly relieved when the scenes are over. I know the text is
important, and she has something desperately important to say to
Gertrude — but first one has to get over the fact that we do have a

backlog of knowledge of that play that can get in the way. The most important things she says are in the first lines to Gertrude; and therefore we must arrest the audience's attention very quickly or we're going to have lost that. We have an Ophelia who is everything that is described in the text, but I was a little worried by the delicacy of her hands, and for no reason that I can find tried tying her hands to a lady-in-waiting, to see if that would produce an extra effort of frustration or energy or necessity to communicate harder the text to the Queen, when the hands couldn't get in the way, being mad. It didn't work entirely, it produced a vague effect. I then asked for a stick and we tied her hands, like with a yoke on her shoulders and her hands were tied over the sides. And that had an extraordinary effect on the rest of the company. It produced the possibility that she was dangerous in her lunacy, that unless her hands were in some way restricted she could damage herself, let alone others. It also became a very dangerous weapon, because the ends sticking out (if she turned too sharply) could hit another character in the face. So she became not only the possible danger, because there was obviously some reason why she needed to be restricted, but also there was the physical danger of what she could do with that device to other people. That has now been carried forward into a design that is totally fabricated in the sense of an Elizabethan strait-jacket. It's a very beautiful object, very like a yoke for carrying milk-pails, made of ebony inlaid with silver with finials in silver at the ends, velvet padding where it sits on the neck, immaculate strapping with silver buckles that brace it around the body. But it has nothing to with historical accuracy, it's a totally imaginative creation that galvanizes the scenes into something that allows Ophelia to stay on stage long enough to say all the things that she says, and for our attention to be arrested firmly enough for us to want to listen to what she has to say.

I guess that with a lot of my productions I will have 'gimmick' hurled at me, which seems to happen all the time, and it seems to me that a 'gimmick' is something that has no justification and that is lightly conceived. I don't think that I've ever done a production that has been lightly conceived. Nothing, whether it be sitting beside a pool (in *Two Gentlemen*) or this particular gadget for Ophelia, comes without a great deal of consideration. It would have remained just a rehearsal technique and never have got into the production unless it had proved to support or in some way assist the sharing with the audience whatever the given thought is. That's always the hard decision about any idea that comes from the text — yes, they start from there, but you eventually get beyond. How far beyond can you go before you are padding the text rather than supporting it? I don't care what it is, if it produces the direct contact between actor and audience so that they are spontaneously arriving at a scene together, then any trick should stay in a production. Even if it's as anachronistic as a car suddenly driving into the middle of a Renaissance production, I don't care, if it makes you at that point listen to a line of text that you can't achieve in any other way. God forbid that one should drive a car into a Renaissance play, of course. But the light-hearted, the cavalier attitude in which a new thought is referred to as a 'gimmick' is very alarming; it's pretty obvious when something is a gimmick or a considered, illuminating effect. It may not be necessary for certain scholars to have that part of the text illuminated, or pointed out, or explained. But you don't direct plays for scholars. I direct plays for a fourteen-year-old of either sex who's never been to the theatre before, and I want them to understand it, I want them to experience something remarkable for the first time. If I achieve that, the majority of my audience will share a similar experience.

RB There's no reason whatsoever why the text at a given point should not crystallise into a physical embodiment, an icon, of the energies which are generally expressed in that situation. And such a happening doesn't deserve to be called a 'gimmick'. It's clear, for instance, that the situation of madness and needed restraint in which Ophelia finds herself can logically be realised in the piece of apparatus which you've created for her. I would judge this to be far more effective with audiences than the set-piece, recital-type Mad Scene of Ophelia – which, let's admit it, is more or less a cliché of *Hamlet* productions, and which I myself on many occasions have found extremely unmoving. Now this is a subjective fact, and I suspect that this is a collective fact for others too.

RP There's the other one, that is marvellously performed, where you are so in awe of the remarkable talent that has produced this detailed and realistic creation of madness that you are only admiring the acting. There are some scenes where the text is full enough for the point to be made, but when wretched Ophelia comes on and in the first few lines says – it's the only occasion in the play when anyone says it – those incredible lines to Gertrude, 'How should I your true love know/From another one?' Will I know him by his clothes, or will I know him by an unnatural grave? – it must alarm Gertrude no end. How will I know your first husband from your second husband? By his dress, or by a grave that suggests some unnatural death? She says that at the beginning of the scene. It's the most important thing she says in the scene, the only time that Gertrude is given an inkling of what's happened before the play begins. And if you're not careful, it's gone and over in either a fascination with the technique of the actress, or, as you say, thinking 'O God here's that dreary scene where the girl skips around and looks pathetic.' If we can arrive at a point when the first image is so alarming that that arrests our attention, by the time she starts the first dialogue we are absolutely with her. Then we've got a fighting chance. That's the important thing about the scene, to get that first line over. It's a great help that she has to sing!

RB With that image – I've long had a theory that what's important in drama is what the audience remembers, after it's forgotten everything else. I find that I can usually remember, years after, just one or two major moments. But these images that I retain are always significant, and they always seem retroactively to govern the production in my mind. And I'm sure that this can be said of the image of the poor Ophelia tied to this gilded yoke, which even as you describe it is to me immensely pathetic and moving. How much more must it seem to the audience in the theatre?

RP I agree about images. If the image exactly matches the text, as with the instance in *Measure for Measure*. After the big duologue between Angelo and Isabella, in our production Isabella is left with this incredible proposition. Martha Henry, heaving partly from fright, partly possibly from an unsuspected excitement, but in what is usually an ice-cold scene, dipped her hands into a water-jug that is on the desk and splashed cold water on to her forehead and we knew she was hot. And it seems to me that to be left with the image that this glacial, white-dressed, pure virgin is *hot* is a crystallisation of what the scene is about. And if that is what is remembered, in fact people are also remembering the text, because every ounce of the text leads you to that action. The almost unbearable bewilderment at the end is that of decision. She does not, as we are told by many essayists, marry the Duke. She may, after the play, but she doesn't in Shakespeare's play. She neither accepts nor rejects him. From the text, we assume that she doesn't accept him, because he repeats the offer. But she doesn't say anything, so we are left to make up our own minds. The pivoting figure of Isabella in our production, as she slowly turned, removing her glasses, and then her nun's head-dress, and finally the back of the hand just resting on the forehead, but at the same time the body never stopped turning, but just spinning before our eyes seems to me to be exactly what that silence is saying. If Shakespeare wanted to say that she accepts the Duke, he would have said it. If he wanted to say that she rejects him, he would have said it. But she says nothing. We are left with a bewilderment, with an ambiguity, with a woman who has not yet decided one way or the other. And it seems to me that if that is the image that is left, it is also the embodiment of what the text (or the lack of text for her) is saying. If it's the right image, it will also be finally the text that you're remembering.

RB The search then is for the necessary image, that accords with the most scrupulous fidelity with the text and communicates this remembered text to the audience.

May I ask you, now, what Shakespeare play you would like to direct? It's clear from the tenor of our conversation that this isn't a throwaway question, it's the logical extension of everything that we've been talking about.

RP I want to direct *A Winter's Tale*. I'd like to direct *The Tempest* that I think Shakespeare wanted to write, which isn't the same as saying I'd like to direct *The Tempest*. I am in fact at the moment directing *The Tempest*, but I have a terrible feeling that it isn't quite the play he wanted to write; I think he gets caught up with the fashion of his own time, and gets trapped in the middle of perhaps his most remarkable freedom with Elizabethan masque-work, at just the moment when he appears about to break beyond the bounds of even his genius. But I think that most of all at the moment I want to direct *A Winter's Tale*. I don't know when I will. I'm pleased to be doing the ones I am doing, and I think that the ones I'm doing at the moment have something new to say, something new to experience. And I hope and pray that I won't have very often to direct the ones that just come around again because it's time they came round again.

RB And that leads me to my final question: what are your ambitions for the Stratford Shakespearean Festival?

RP I would like Stratford to see its position in the graph of a theatre nationally. I would like other theatres in Canada to see their position in that graph as related to Stratford. I would like Stratford eventually to know its audience.

GIORGIO STREHLER

Ralph Berry I'd like to begin by asking you about Shakespeare and Italy. If we exclude England — and Shakespeare sets his plays in England only when he is virtually compelled to — the country that he most frequently selects is Italy. It is a fact that Shakespeare sets many of his plays in Italy, of his own choice. Now this must be significant. It is not simply a matter of Italy being an exciting, exotic, interesting background. It's clear that Shakespeare has a great feeling for locale in his plays. So I put it, then: the Italian element is important in Shakespeare. And I ask, how do you respond to the Italian element?

    Giorgio Strehler The question is important, and difficult to resolve. The problem of locality in Shakespeare, whether in the Roman plays or in the other tragedies or comedies set in Italy, is critical. One has to search for Shakespeare's reasons in choosing to set so many plays in Italy. Much has been written on this: obviously, I don't have a complete answer, for it's one of the fundamental issues with Shakespeare. For instance, there's the primary problem of knowing what were the direct relations between Shakespeare and Italy. If Shakespeare was a butcher's son, it's certain that he never knew Italy directly, that he had never seen a town in Italy. And perhaps one wonders if it is possible that the William Shakespeare whom tradition describes to us could ever have known Italy (directly or indirectly) through the available cultural sources. Now, I would say quite simply of the mysteries in this phenomenon of Shakespeare, that one knows what it is necessary to know, that is to say, one knows what he wrote. And the fact is that he gave, miraculously, a different accent to a play unfolding in one country rather than another.

    That is not a question of poetic intuition, you understand; one can intuitively comprehend the general character of England, or if you like the general character of an Italian or Frenchman. It's rather broad, but not too difficult to grasp. I can talk about America with you, but except for a month I've never been there. All the same, I have some insight into what America is. I am not absolutely convinced, though, that I understand the difference between someone living in Tennessee and in Alabama. That would be an affair not of culture but of poetic intuition. One needs poetic intuition to be able to write a play like *Romeo and Juliet*, which takes place in Verona, and create an impres-

sion of the events, the characters, and the townsfolk generally which
has a terrible exactitude and reality; and all this in a small part of
one town in a country of 45 million inhabitants (of course, there were
many fewer then). It's something I've often thought about, the character of a nation or of a town like Verona. There's a character-type
that is found in this part of Italy, which has a tendency to extreme
violence and to behaviour just like that of the Capulets and Mont-
agues, the two houses continually at odds. These people are excit-
able, hot-blooded. It's a regional characteristic, though I don't say
that all the inhabitants of Verona are like that. But if one takes up the
story of Romeo and Juliet, and sets it in Italy, in Verona, that is
certainly more appropriate than placing it in Turin, or Milan, or Venice.
The precision of Shakespeare's poetic intuition is inexplicable. We know
well enough that *Romeo and Juliet* was taken from a novel – I don't
recall its name – a tale of the period when this town had two leading
houses. But this inner acquaintance with the character of a small town,
that is something that one can only have if one has lived there with
its people, truly knows the place. If one has merely met two or three
people from Italy, that is insufficient. So that's the problem, and it's
a large one.

RB I think I phrased the original question rather badly, because
strictly speaking Shakespeare does not write about Italy at all. He
writes about Venice, Verona, Milan, particular locations with a particular character. Shakespeare is always trying to create a local society,
a society which explains and accounts for the events that go on. As you
say, the events that make up *Romeo and Juliet* could only have occurred
in Verona. They could not have occurred in Venice, because the Venetians are not hot-blooded.

GS That reveals the artist. The tragic events in Shakespeare are
of such magnitude that it cannot be said that a play like *Romeo and
Juliet* could not happen in Venice. That is possible – certainly, there
were families and characters who could have been close enough to
that. But the grandeur of Shakespeare cannot be restricted in this
way. It's impossible, for instance, to think that Prospero should not be
Duke of Milan in the romance, if Prospero is Duke of Turin. It's the
same thing. Again, *Othello* could have been set in Naples, shall we say.

Othello is a particularly clear issue, illuminated by the constitution
of Venetian society. A tragedy like *Coriolanus* (or *Julius Caesar*) is
based on Roman history, but there are things in it that could have
happened anywhere. Now this is not the case with *Macbeth*, which
takes place in a certain era in a certain part of Britain; it's necessary

to place the tragedy in an ambience nearest to what the drama seeks to signify. That is to say, when Shakespeare sets *King Lear* in a country and an era which is not precisely indicated, it is exactly because these matters must be left vague. It's understood that *King Lear* is set in a distant epoch. It's a kind of Biblical tragedy, shall we say an archetype of tragedy, more so than *Hamlet*, which takes place in Elsinore. Now it's exactly right for *Hamlet* to take place in Elsinore.

RB How, as a director, do you seek to realise the society, the national background or ambience? For instance, in *King Lear,* as you say, the place and time are vague, distant. How did you devise sets and costumes for *King Lear*?

GS When Shakespeare provides the ambience of one country or another, he has good reason for doing so. He always finds the exact context, of geographical and national character, for the drama that he is going to write. And for the historical era, too. So one question is place and the other is time. I think that the Roman plays are Roman plays, even if the general character of Shakespeare's work is Elizabethan. There is always a partial vision of a certain moment in history. Now, you ask about the realisation of Shakespeare's plays: nowadays a director must preoccupy himself with historical reality. If, to represent this problem, one takes all the plays about kings, which are obviously the most historically defined — *Richard II, Henry V, Henry VI,* and so on — one calls these plays 'The Kings' because they make up a part of English history. But I ask myself if it is necessary to set *Richard II* in the time of Richard II. It is idiotic to dress the Scots in kilts, for instance, though I have always seen it done. The plays of Shakespeare should be staged always in the *type* in which they should be displayed. One solution is to dress the *dramatis personae* in Elizabethan costume. Now, I think it an error to present *Julius Caesar* in Roman costume, just as it is an error to put *Richard II* in English costume, to make the face of Richard II resemble somewhat the historical Richard who is buried in Westminster. There are two poles: it's an error to choose Elizabethan costume, and it's an error to stage *Hamlet* or *Julius Caesar* in contemporary costume. Julius Caesar has been presented as Mussolini, for instance, and I recall Alec Guinness as a contemporary Hamlet and Orson Welles' *Julius Caesar* at the Guild Theatre in America. The question, then, relates to the twin problems of setting and critical interpretation. Today we have progressed further in actualising and historicising Shakespeare. An orientation must be found for each play that is not solely one of costume: an ambience, a setting which corresponds to the profundity of the piece.

RB Could you illustrate this from your work?

GS Well, I've staged eight, ten plays of Shakespeare — I really don't remember. For twenty-five years it's been a path to knowledge with Shakespeare. The point is that it doesn't correspond with what I think today. The record of my productions is simply a process of learning.

RB Very well, your latest production, then. Tell me about that.

GS When I produced *Julius Caesar* I created a setting which was passionately historical, with Roman costumes. That is gone today. I would not have done anything else, you understand. I did it because at that moment, I saw no other possibility of doing it differently. To take another instance, I produced *Richard III* in Elizabethan costume, but today I would no longer choose a setting which resembled a re-construction of the Elizabethan theatre. When I did *Richard II*, I created an abstract setting, a symbolic, poetic abstract of the Eliza-bethan stage. Because at that moment, five years ago, we were obses-sed by the Elizabethan stage. Today I would not do it. I set *King Lear* in an empty stage, where one could think of a kind of metaphysical circus, with a cyclorama. One entered into a stage of plastic material. And there were very few words for decorative purposes. The stage for *Lear* was based on Eliot's *The Waste Land* — the ambience of the production was that of the poem. It was an empty plain which could be the terrestrial planet, or a cosmic circus, where this event at once very ancient and close to us took place. The actors were clad in the manner of the Italian Renaissance, but all in black leather. In my imagination they were personages of Shakespeare's time, but trans-posed with people who could have been motor-cyclists of today. The kings, Lear and the others, were dressed in long theatrical robes, with crowns of paper.

RB Paper crowns?

GS Crowns made of gold paper. The style is eclectic. Eclecticism, be it understood, has positive or negative possibilities. Now, I see Shakes-peare as a poet who surpasses the age in which he is enclosed, but at the same time is bound to it. He is at once national, English, Eliza-bethan, and universal. That is the central fact that one has to interpret. It's too easy to make Hamlet come on dressed as a young man of today, or the Ghost dressed in something military with a mask. It's just as easy to do that as it is to mount *Hamlet* in Elizabethan costume. Given that the play is set in Elsinore, in Denmark, should Hamlet have blonde hair (because he's a 'Dane') and be dressed in black? We've moved beyond those things, which are no more than a kind of heritage of

Romanticism, and a species of naturalism applied to Shakespeare. Shakespeare breaks out of this schema; and for each of his works one must find the precise ambience which is contained not in the stage directions, but in the lexicon of the piece itself.

RB You spoke of the historic moment in Shakespeare, and you obviously have a very acute sense of time and place in Shakespeare. Can we go beyond that, and consider history itself in Shakespeare? I'm thinking particularly of the eight plays of English history, which run in order of composition from *Henry VI* to *Henry V*. You have been concerned a great deal with Shakespeare's history plays, and I'd like to ask: do you consider that a certain view of history emerges from these plays?

GS Yes. It's an enormous problem, Shakespeare is a continent: there's the problem of history, of man with himself, of man in love ... One must try to attain a broad vision of Shakespeare. But history is a specific issue. One has to ask, 'What is happening?' of all the plays in the canon; because the sense of history is not, as I think, confined to the King-plays, or those plays which are classified as 'histories'. History is present in all his plays. But what do we derive from this sense of history? Very well, there's a vision of history, of a certain pessimistic cast. Pessimist, but not despairing, because Shakespeare is always *active*. The pessimist of tragic vision of Shakespeare is never absolutely negative. He's not a Beckett. There is, however, a kind of conviction of the corruption latent in power.

RB I'm fascinated by your remark about the pessimistic vision of Shakespeare. I was thinking of the curious fact that he begins writing his history plays with *Henry VI*, which tells of a social and national disaster, and then he goes on to *Henry V*, the last in the sequence, which tells of a brilliant success. But in the chronology of English history, the reign of Henry V comes before Henry VI.

GS Immediately before.

RB Immediately before, so therefore what emerges is a kind of cycle, a cycle that goes from the disaster of Henry VI to the triumph of Henry V. But we know that the triumph will again be followed by disaster.

GS Yes, I think that's understood.

RB So does this suggest a cyclic view of history?

GS Cyclic, yes. It's a circle of history. But when I spoke of a pessimistic vision, I wanted to say also a dialectical vision. It's not a pessimistic vision which offers no possibility of issue. Shakespeare finds himself, I think, in a situation when Henry V could be a glorification of a king whom Shakespeare as an Englishman loved well, or who was at that moment necessary for a glorification of his country. At which point Henry is as virtuous as Richard II is a monster. Perhaps all the plays of Shakespeare are to be seen as a grand allegory of history in which all those with power are kings, who kill each other for power, the power which corrupts. It's a process from which the people are absent. Apart from *Hamlet*, the only revolt on stage in Shakespeare is Jack Cade's rebellion, is it not? But all these forces are seeking a power which corrupts and hates and at the same time may close the bloody circle of history. Now Shakespeare could not fail to perceive this enduring element of human history. The question is whether Shakespeare's vision perceived a point of exit, and that is hard. My view is that Shakespeare had a pessimistic vision of history, but not a pessimistic vision of man.

RB But you spoke a moment ago of the dialectic of history. Are not the implications of dialectic basically positive, optimistic if you like?

GS Myself, I'm a Socialist, with a materialistic view of history, I'm a Marxist; so I believe personally in developing the dialectic in a positive sense. But the dialectic itself is neither positive nor negative. Dialectic is dialectic, it's thesis and antithesis, that which is balanced in the movement of history. I happen to believe in a positive development in the movement of human thought. He did not, surely, believe in a blind movement of history, a process where one murder succeeded another. I think that Shakespeare always let it be understood in his tragedies that man himself had his rights even against history, or in dialectic with history. All the great personages of Shakespeare are in dialectic with history, with fetishes of power and with fetishes. What is *Macbeth* but the inner dialectic of Macbeth in the fifth Act, 'Tomorrow and tomorrow and tomorrow . . .'?

RB I'm going to suggest that Shakespeare's last history play was *The Tempest*. I don't know if you'd agree with that; but if you do, I'd like to ask you, what is the verdict that comes at the end of *The Tempest*?

GS It's undoubtedly Shakespeare's last play, in the sense that he terminates a certain poetic course. I would suggest that *The Tempest* is, indeed, a résumé of his entire work. In *The Tempest* one finds as in the memory a repetition of all the dramatic situations which run, if you like, from *Romeo and Juliet* to *Macbeth*. But what conclusion is one to infer from this?

RB I had in mind this particular difficulty: *The Tempest* is very much concerned with the problems of power, of how people are governed. But the play ends with a kind of open-ended question. Prospero knows how to govern, but he is going to die. What will happen? Will Ferdinand and Miranda, those nice children, be able to govern and succeed? Or will Sebastian and Antonio, who are still there, be able to take over? Then there's the question of Caliban at the end.

GS Prospero gives Ariel his liberty. But what does he do with Caliban? It's a question that has always given me intense perplexity.

RB So the real question is what will happen when Prospero dies? What will happen to history?

GS It's certain that Prospero abandons power. But not only power: he abandons all the powers of his being, even the power of enchantment, which is to say the power of becoming a poet. He has broken his staff, and Ariel will not come back. It's a pessimistic position, which makes this statement: Now I will retire, and I have ended my power. It's yours, to go forward. Prospero has not only set aside power, he has decided to think only of his death.

RB '. . . where Every third thought shall be my grave.'

GS He's a man who says, no more writing, no more making poems. Now, one must consider the people who are going to live. Shakespeare, I am certain, always had an enormous confidence in the coming generation. At the last, Shakespeare breaks his magic wand and permits the young people to depart, one of them the thing most dear to him – his daughter – and the other, a young prince. They are most like the couple from Pamino in *The Magic Flute*, the pairing of Adam and Eve to renew the world. You ask if they will be capable of that renewal. Prospero says, 'Are you capable of carrying on before history and against these forces and these limits?' But he, who could command and see truly, will not be present. That is an agonising question, concerning Shakespeare's vision at that moment in his life. What did he think? Evidently, he no longer had the strength to fight against the destiny of man. He had already done what he could.

RB So Prospero's final appeal to the audience is a statement that the future is over to you, the future is with you. You must decide.

GS That's exactly what I think. He says, 'Over to you now.'

RB That's not really pessimistic, neither is it optimistic. It's a simple statement that you must make society work.

GS Precisely. That's to say, to the pessimist vision Shakespeare gives always a point of optimism, a point of possibility. There is a universe, let's say Beckett's – I don't want to set up a Beckett/Shakespeare opposition – which is clearly restricted to oneself, it's finished. Shakespeare always leaves the possibility of the decision with the coming generation and the society which is going to make itself. It's always projected to the future. The circle is never absolutely closed in itself.

RB If I have understood you rightly, then, you regard the work of Shakespeare as a statement of human possibilities?

GS Yes, yes.

RB Can I ask you, finally, what is Shakespeare for you today?

GS In all the panorama of dramatic poetry in the world, there's a choice which is personal, one of taste. It has to do with the personality of each director. Myself, I have staged the work of Chekhov, Goldoni, Molière, and so on. Amongst the phenomena of world drama, Shakespeare holds a special place. Why? Because Shakespeare, of all the great dramatic poets, had the largest, most universal vision. Naturally, there are some problems which present themselves to humanity which are not reflected in Shakespeare's work. But one finds always the possibility of speaking to contemporary audiences of problems which pierce us today through something that Shakespeare has written. What I find in Shakespeare is contemporaneity. I produce Shakespeare because he is my contemporary.

PETER BROOK

Ralph Berry In *The Empty Space* you wrote, 'In the second half of the twentieth century in England . . . we are faced with the infuriating fact that Shakespeare is still our model.' I wonder if you would like to modify now either the general proposition, or perhaps the word 'infuriating'?

Peter Brook No, it is infuriating, and infuriating in a very good way, because it would be nice to feel that we could do as well. Everything after all is a product of its times to a large degree — not totally, but to a large degree, and everything that is produced at any moment reflects the quality and understanding of life at that moment; and it's quite clear that to find a richer model than the model we can produce ourselves we're forced to look backwards. I think the thing that is infuriating about this is that each generation needs to find its new way, and not refer constantly to given models. Never has that been truer than today, when the whole need is to break out of one set of forms and find new ones. And there's no doubt that today, there is a barrier in accepting something, however valid, however truth-containing, if its outside form reflects the past. And that's why one puts the real accent on the word 'infuriating'. There are thousands of people for whom a playhouse, in which the imagery is to do with kings and queens and goddesses, is virtually intolerable. Now I don't think we have to discuss the rights and wrongs of this — it may be childish, it may be ridiculous, but it's certainly one of the factors that makes the meaning and the potential life-giving qualities of the performances of Shakespeare's works handicapped compared with the lesser qualities that come through in an electronic, science-fiction, crash-helmeted idiom.

RB So, the fact remains though for reasons on the one hand of a genetic accident, the birth of Shakespeare, and on the other hand the immense cultural convulsions that we're going through, he remains the one playwright that one has to face up to, who is alone in his league.

PB Of all time.

RB It seems to me that the most immediate way in which Shakespeare impresses himself upon us generally, and upon you as director particularly, is in the choice of his plays for performance. I know that this isn't always true. Someone who's directing a summer season, a festival season let's say, will have to have a pretty good reason for not producing *Twelfth Night* or some such crowd-puller. But a man in your position is able to select only the Shakespeare play that he wishes, at that moment in history, to produce. Now could you enlarge on some of the reasons that lead you to select, of this rather large canon, one play at a given moment when presumably you feel that this is the moment, this is the right play for now?

PB That's a vast, and in a way absolutely marvellous question, because through this question (I don't think there's any other) everything is brought into relief. I think that through it one can see perhaps the great misunderstanding that hangs over Shakespearian works, but I'd be very interested to try to answer it. To begin with, I don't think I can face the question without dwelling for a moment on what Shakespeare is. As you said very rightly a moment ago, he is alone in his league. And I think that one of the things that is very little understood about Shakespeare is that he is not only of a different quality, he is also different in kind. And this is very little understood. So long as one thinks that Shakespeare is just Ionesco but better, Beckett but richer, Brecht but more human, Chekhov with crowds, and so on, one is not touching what it's all about. If you can talk about cats and a bull, one sees that these are different species. In modern scientific analysis you would beware of the dangers of mixing categories, and talking about a person in category A as though he really belonged to category B. I think that this is what happens with Shakespeare in relation to other playwrights, and so I'd like to dwell for a moment on what this particular phenomenon is.

To me, this phenomenon is very simple. It is that authorship as we understand it in almost all other fields — in the way that one talks about the authorship of a book or poem, and today the authorship of a film when directors are called authors of their films, and so on — almost invariably means 'personal expression'. And therefore the finished work bears the marks of the author's own way of seeing life. It's a cliché of criticism that one comes across very often, 'his world', 'the world of this author'. Now it's not for nothing that scholars who have tried so hard to find autobiographical traces in Shakespeare have had so little success. It doesn't matter in fact who wrote the plays and what biographical traces there are. The fact is that there is singularly little of the author's point of view — and his personality seems to be very hard to seize — throughout thirty-seven or thirty-eight plays. Now if one takes those thirty-seven plays with all the radar lines of the

different viewpoints of the different characters, one comes out with a
field of incredible density and complexity; and eventually one goes a
step further, and one finds that what happened, what passed through
this man called Shakespeare and came into existence on sheets of
paper, is something quite different from any other author's work. It's
not Shakespeare's view of the world, it's something which actually
resembles reality. A sign of this is that any single word, line, character
or event has not only a large number of interpretations, but an unlimited number. Which is the characteristic of reality. I could say that
is the characteristic of any action in the real world — say, the action
that you're doing now at this moment as we are talking together of
putting your hand against your head. An artist may try to capture and
reflect your action, but actually he interprets it — so that a naturalistic painting, a Picasso painting, a photograph, are all interpretations.
But in itself, the action of one man touching his head is open to
unlimited understanding and interpretation. In reality, that is. What
Shakespeare wrote carries that characteristic. What he wrote is not
interpretation: it is the thing itself.

   And if we're very bold, and think not in very constricting verbal
terms, 'he's an author, he wrote plays, the plays have scenes' and so
on, but think much more broadly and say 'this creator created an
enormous skein of interrelated words', and if we think of a chain of
several hundred thousand words unfolding in a certain order, the whole
making an extraordinary fabric, I think that then one begins to see
the essential point. And that is that this fabric reaches us today, not as
a series of messages, which is what authorship almost always produces
— it is a series of impulses that can produce many understandings.
This is something quite different. It is like tea-leaves in a cup. Think
of the chance arrangement of tea-leaves in a cup — the act of interpretation is a reflection of what is brought to the cup by the person
looking at it. The whole act of interpreting tea-leaves — of interpreting
the fall of a sparrow, for that matter — is the unique meeting, at one
point in time, between an event and the perceiver of the event.

   I think that two things come out of it. On the one hand, it is obvious
that every interpretation of this material is a subjective act — how else
could it be? — and that each person, whether it's a scholar writing, an
actor acting, a director directing or a designer designing, brings to it
and always has and always will his subjectivity. Which means that
even if he tries to bridge the ages and say, 'I leave myself and my
century behind, and I'm looking at it with the eyes of its own period',
one knows that this is nonsense, and nothing bears this out more

vividly than the history of stage costume, which shows more than anything else two periods at once. The designer tries to interpret one period and is not aware of the elements of his own moment that he's also bringing — so he produces a double image. We look at Granville-Barker's productions — or we look at any production anywhere — and the double image is always there. This is an unavoidable human fact, each person brings what he is; there's no man walking around this world that's somehow dropped his ego. How you use your ego is the question. You can wilfully and blindly give your ego free rein, or you can put your ego into play in a way that can help the truth to appear. For instance, the history of leading acting. The actor who's the crude, bombastic, self-inflated type seizes on Shakespeare's plays because he sees, in their million facets, the facets which are food for his 'me'. He certainly gets a powerful energy out of what he finds, and the demonstration may be dazzling. But the play has gone, and the finer content, and many other levels of meaning are steam-rollered out of existence. Of course, the theatre artist's relations with his material are basically affective, they come out of a love for and affinity with what he's doing. Doing a play as a duty, even on the highest level of duty, won't work. The mysterious and essential creative channels will not be opened, and so he will only be able to call on his reason, he won't actually be able to bring out the fullest and richest possibilities to bear. So obviously for a director as for an actor there is a moment that is purely instinctive and affective that makes the decision to do a certain play. And this is something that must be respected. In the same way, you don't beyond a point force an actor to play a part that he doesn't want to do; you don't coax people into working in a play that they have an antipathy for, and so on. On the other hand, the danger that also has to be watched is when any of the artists or scholars dealing with a play of Shakespeare allow their love and excitement and enthusiasm to blind them to the fact that their interpretation can never be complete. There's an enormous danger that takes very precise form; and if that's forgotten, one gets into a form of acting that one's seen over many years, a form of directing, a form of designing, which proudly presents very subjective versions of the play without a glimmer of awareness that this might be diminishing the play — on the contrary, a vain belief that this is the play and more — not only Shakespeare's play, but Shakespeare's play as made into sense by such-and-such an individual. And that's where the virtue of having a feeling of love and enthusiasm has to be tempered by a cool sense that anybody's personal view of the play is bound to be less than the play itself.

I saw the other day an interview on French television with Orson Welles, on Shakespeare, where he started by saying something like 'We all betray Shakespeare.' The history of the plays shows them constantly being re-interpreted and re-interpreted, and yet remaining untouched and intact. Therefore they are always more than the last interpretation trying to say the last word on something on which the last word can't be said.

So to come back to your essential question: all the plays of Shakespeare that I've done, I've done for no other reason than that I've wanted to, very strongly. On the other hand, over the years my own view of what I'm doing and why has changed enormously. The very first production of Shakespeare that I did was *Love's Labour's Lost*, I think, and at that point I felt and believed the work of a director was to have a vision of a play and to 'express' it. I thought that's what a director was for. That was how I understood directing at that time – I was nineteen or twenty. I had always wanted to direct films, and in fact I started in films before going into the theatre. A film director shows his pictures to the world, and I thought a stage director did the same in another way. Even before I did *Love's Labour's Lost*, when I was up at Oxford I terribly wanted to do *Coriolanus*, and I remember very strongly that the way of wanting to do *Coriolanus* was sitting at a table and drawing pictures. I drew images of *Coriolanus*, which is the film director's way of wanting to bring into life a personal picture one has, a picture of Coriolanus walking away in brilliant sunlight, things like that. When I did *Love's Labour's Lost* I had a set of images in mind, which I wanted to bring to life just like making a film. So *Love's Labour's Lost* was a very visual, very romantic set of stage pictures which I then did in a Watteau costume, eighteenth-century Romantic manner. And I remember that from then all the way through to *Measure for Measure* my conviction was that the director's job, having found an affinity between himself and the play, was to find the images that he believed in and through them make the play live for a contemporary audience. In this sense he was always a man of his time. In an image-conscious time. I believed designing and directing to be inseparable. A good designer – in any field – has to sense just how the shapes are for a particular moment, and therefore produces the right car body, and so on. In exactly the same way I understood that a director studies deeply, is as in tune with the play as he can be, but that his work is the making of a new set of images for it. Since then, this view has changed, evolved, through a growing awareness that the total overall image was so much less than the play itself. And eventually, as I worked more and more outside proscenium theatres and in the forms of theatre where the overall image proved to be less and less necessary and important, it became clear that a play of Shakespeare, and therefore a production of Shakespeare, could go far beyond the unity that one man's image could give, beyond that of the director and designer. And it was only through discovering that there was far more to it than that, that my interest moved from liking the play, and therefore showing my image of the play, to another process, which starts always with the instinctive feeling that this is the play for now.

This is a big change of attitude: without thinking consciously or analytically in these terms, a sense that this play is meaningful in many ways at this moment opens my awareness. It's not only that it's meaningful for me autobiographically at this moment. At certain points in one's life one can identify with and wish to do a youthful play, a bitter play, a tragic play – this is fine, but one can then go beyond to see how a whole area of living experience that seems close to one's own concerns is also close to the concerns of the people in the world around one. When these elements come together, then is the time to do that play, and not another.

Fortunately, I've never been in the position of having to do lots of plays systematically. I think it's always destructive, to have to do plays in this way. I started with wanting to do certain plays, which I directed, and not being interested by certain authors. For years I wanted to do *Lear*, and I did it; for years I wanted to do *Antony and Cleopatra*, and I haven't. I never wanted to do a *Twelfth Night* – these are purely personal things, I think that every director has them that way, plays he's more drawn to, and every actor has. But I would now say that that's our loss; choosing plays is a Rorschach test by which you can tell the openness and blinkeredness of each individual. Because if I could sympathise and empathise with every one of Shakespeare's plays, and every one of his themes, and every one of his characters, I would be that much the richer, and I think that goes for any actor. And if a theatre were to take on the task of doing the entire work of Shakespeare, out of an absolute conviction that this is the greatest school of living that they know, that group would be an astonishing group in human terms, because the mere fact of being able to do that would be an action of penetration and understanding. In the very first instance, I think one must be led to a play by certain instincts which at the same time reflect something of one's times – it's a violent play at a violent moment, or a joyful play at a moment when one needs joy.

A fuller attitude begins to shape itself when there is not only a response
of the ego, of the personality, to what it likes and dislikes, but when
there's a response of the personality to what it can discover through
working on the play; and this is a very big step, because as long as
one's in the first instinct, 'I like this, I want to do it', one is most
likely within the closed circle of wishing to illustrate what one likes.
'I like it, and I'll show you why I like it.' The next step is, 'I like it,
because it parallels all that I need to know about in the world.' If I
spend three months on a play, at the end of that time my wish to understand will have taken me further along through its complexity, and in
the same way will take an audience eventually on the same experience.
And thus, from personal expression as an aim, you go to shared discovery.

RB May I take up a couple of points there? First, when you were
talking of image-making, I thought of your *Love's Labour's Lost*, and
I'd like to refer to the great theatrical moment in the play, in the
entrance of Mercade. Could you elaborate on the way this was staged?

PB If I remember rightly, I was struck by what seemed to me to be
self-evident, but which at the time seemed to be unheard-of: which
was, that from the moment Mercade came on, the whole play changed
its tone entirely, because he came into an artificial world to announce
a piece of news that was real. He came on bringing death. And as I felt
intuitively that the image of the Watteau world was very close to this,
I began to see that the reason that the Watteau 'Age of Gold' is so particularly moving is that although it's a picture of springtime, it's an
autumn springtime, because every one of Watteau's pictures has an
incredible melancholy. And if one looks, one sees that there is somewhere in it the presence of death, until one even sees that in Watteau
(unlike the imitators of the period, where it's all sweetness and pretti-
ness) there is usually a dark figure somewhere, standing with his back to
you, and some people say that he is Watteau himself. But there's no
doubt that the dark touch gives the dimension to the whole piece.
And it was through this that I brought Mercade over the rise at the
back of the stage — it was evening, the lights were going down, and
suddenly over it came a man in black. And the man in black on a very
pretty summery stage, with everybody in pale pastel Watteau and Lan-
cret costumes and golden light dying, and suddenly over the skyline
coming this figure in black was very disturbing, and at once something
in the whole audience was felt.

RB This presence embodies a reality which has gradually been
making itself felt in very complex ways throughout the play, a reality

assuming mass and direction in the later stages which finally material-
ises in this.

Could I also go back to what you were saying about the wholeness
of the canon? It seems to me that one of the great difficulties of
interpretation is that when we look at the apparent objects before us,
that is to say a text of Shakespeare, our view is going to change if we
take it in relation to other plays around it in the canon. For instance, if
we come to *Twelfth Night* chronologically, via *Much Ado* and *As You
Like It*, it will appear to us in a certain way. If we come to it backwards,
via *Troilus and Cressida* and *All's Well*, it assumes a different reality —
the play of lights and shadows falls from a different angle.

PB Which is what Peter Hall brought out by playing the histories
in the order of the canon. I think that's absolutely true, but I think
that what you're putting your finger on there is still another way of
seeing the endlessly moving, endlessly changing, unique nature of this
material. The plays in themselves seem, falsely, to be static things
because you see them on a shelf — a real naïveté of vision! One says,
'if that book's on a shelf, I'll go out of the room, I'll come back and it
will still be there,' and it's still there — therefore one believes it's static.
It isn't. I've just been reading Tarzan to my little son, and when Tarzan
first discovered a book he saw little squiggles on a page, and he felt
they were little bugs. And he looked at them: 'what are these little
bugs?' and he came back and there were more little bugs. It's marvellously right, because I think that Shakespeare's plays, deceptively
in hard covers, are big bugs within which there are smaller and smaller
bugs. And when the grown-ups go to bed, they move.

I'll give you two examples. I've been working in France on a translation of *Timon of Athens*, for the French. Because they think in
schematic terms always, and because they know very little about
Shakespeare, they — most of the French — have only seen four or
five plays of Shakespeare. They've seen *Coriolanus*, and therefore
they conclude that Shakespeare is a Fascist. He's a great writer, they
say, but he's a Fascist. I know that when they go to see *Timon*, it's
going to be very disturbing, because suddenly this same author, who's
proved to them that he only likes generals who despise the crowd, has
now written a play in which you see that the only sympathetic people
are the honest servants, without money. This is just another version
of the very thing that you're talking about, which is that you can
build a season and make any patchwork of plays, and a whole new set
of bells starts ringing.

This comes out even further working on a translation. I'm working

with a very imaginative, and free, and intelligent French writer, and
constantly we come to a phrase and he says 'What does this mean?
What exactly does this word mean?' He knows English very well, he
brings out a dictionary: does it mean this, or this? And I say: both.
And so in explaining lines to him, we find we work on a page a day.
Because in the explanation, the word begins to take on more and more
dimensions, until he now says, 'Ah, now I understand: the structure of
writing proceeds from *des mots rayonnants*.' I thought this was very
interesting, because that was how he suddenly understood the different
sort of syntax he was trying to translate, finding what words in the
very un-rayonnant nature of French language matched the original.
When you have a word that has these senses, you can see how from it
you can draw a line to the third word or you can draw a line to the
fifth word, or another line to the fifteenth word, and once again you
get into infinite combinations. When I started work in Shakespeare,
I did believe to a limited extent in the possibility of a classical word
music, that each verse had a sound that was correct, with only moderate
variations; and through direct experience I found that this was absolutely and totally untrue. The more musical the approach you bring to
Shakespeare, which means the more sensitive you are to music, the more
you find that there is no way, except by sheer pedantry, that can fix
this line's correct music. It just can't exist. And the more you get into
this, the more you see that an actor who tries to fix his performance is
doing something anti-life. While he has to keep certain consistencies
in what he's doing, or it's just a chaotic performance — within the
central nature of the music each single line as you come back to it
another time re-opens itself to a new music, made round these radiating
points.

    RB 'Des mots rayonnants' is excellent. I think of 'vibrating' as a
way of describing so many words in Shakespeare, in that they cannot
be and should not be restricted to a certain meaning. For instance,
when Cleopatra says of Antony, 'the soldier's pole is fallen', well,
what do we see? A tent-pole, or a may-pole, or the pole star? Do we
see it as phallic in its implications? There are other possibilities, and I
don't even think that we need to establish the priorities there. It's
sufficient to think of the term's vibrations.

    PB I think this is very important, because the great harm done by
scholarship is to try to make choices, and even make quarrels over
who's right and who's wrong, which is what the whole world of foot-
notes has been. Rather, you want endlessly to come back to meeting
this vibration in all its fullness and with all the ambiguity of something

that does change through the ages.

RB It may go even further than this. In the instance I quoted, there is unarguably one word — the textual scholars are happy with 'pole' as the original word, therefore we need only discuss meanings. But so often what textual scholars are discussing is the word itself. And here, I sometimes suspect, we are in the wake of something approximating to a pun with Shakespeare. When, for instance, in *Macbeth* he speaks of the 'temple-haunting martlet' (if it is 'martlet') and then talks (in the Folio) of 'loved Mansonry', how does one emend it?

PB In California today, you'd get great shouts of delight on 'Mansonry'!

RB Anyway, most editors like 'mansionry'. Pope and others prefer 'masonry'. And I think we can see the word as hovering between 'mansionry' and 'masonry'.

PB I think this is absolutely true. And it's very necessary to see the harm that's done when a fixed meaning is established, which is what so much scholarship has done. This is the true scholarship, the way you're speaking of. I was talking the other day of doing what I think would be a marvellous thing, a Shakespeare production with captions on a screen giving a running commentary on every single word. It would be the most hilarious thing, to show the difference between living expression and all this terrible interpretation. Because the harm in the quibble is the implication that Shakespeare was communicating intentions, and therefore we are trying to discover once and for all what the man meant. And the further you go down that road, the nearer madness lies. If on the other hand, you go on the principle of the vibrating word, you then depersonalise in a sense the author. You see Shakespeare not as a communicator but as a creator, you see him creating marvellous objects, like a potter, like sets of earth figures. Now even the most pedantic collector of pre-Columbian art doesn't look at some Mayan figure and try to pin down what the maker of the figure was trying to say. On the contrary, he's up against something where the name and the personality of the maker and what he was trying to say doesn't come into it, although there was a maker. But the figure itself is something that is vibrating with many layers of meaning — everybody dealing with primitive art recognises this. If then one can see that this is a higher level of creation than the 'I communicate my message to you' level, then one perceives that Shakespeare, alone in all playwriting, made plays like those sorts of figures, and that each word is like a little figurine, vibrating with all these layers of meaning. So one comes towards these elements, whether as an actor or director, with a quite

different attitude, quite different relationship. The vibration cannot
take life unless it comes once again into a human organism. So it has
to vibrate through an actor; an actor is not meant to be an empty vessel.
He and the material enter into a momentary fusion. That's perhaps
the great change in our time also, to recognise that an actor is not just
a glove, the actor is *all*. He's partly a channel but he's partly all that
he has lived through, all that he has developed in himself — and the
same goes for the director.

And so one isn't 'serving' Shakespeare. Ever since I started working
with Shakespeare, I've resented one of the idiot clichés that are always
coming up, which is talking about 'serving the author' and 'serving the
play'. My instinct of resentment against this cult of personality is such
that however much I love Shakespeare, the moment I'm told that I'm
serving Shakespeare, there's another instinct that says 'fuck Shakespeare
— why him more than anyone else?' No one in our time actually,
specifically wants to go and serve the Duke of Edinburgh, the Queen,
Shakespeare . . . Now one has to recognise that there is only one service,
which is to the reality which Shakespeare is serving. Then you're
serving something very valid, you're serving the bringing into our
unreal life the elements of reality. And you've got the greatest channel
to it, through the greatest creator in this form, which is Shakespeare.

RB In fact, of course, the phrase that you take exception to is a
formula for somebody's version of Shakespeare.

PB You know, for instance, it was very interesting that with *A
Midsummer Night's Dream*, however well it was received in America,
none the less it caused a resentment because of something that was
very unimportant in England. In England, there was resentment about
the sexual side. That was small but strong — I used to get so many
letters a week about the phallus, regular as clockwork. In America,
with the same big middle-class audience, nothing: because America is
much more attuned, has been attuned for years to nudity, and cocks,
so that nobody, even the matinée ladies, noticed it. Not one letter, not
a postcard. But what the Americans had to swallow was something
that hadn't occurred to the English — Americans complained that
the Company didn't 'look nice'. And where in England it was considered
a vivid young Company, nice young people, working with zest and
enjoyment and not too old for their parts — in America they were
considered a scruffy lot. Even in the papers, people were saying things
like, 'What a pity they're not better-looking', which is always a mean
thing to say about actors, particularly as they're a sexy lot of people
who consider themselves appealing. And then we understood what it

was all about. In America Shakespeare has become such a middle-class, middle-aged, matinée ladies' entertainment, so closely bound to images of gracious living, that a lover in Shakespeare and his girl are assumed to be like Nixon's son-in-law and daughter. Therefore the whole class of people who go to Shakespeare, not knowing what it's all about but feeling somehow that Shakespeare is a part of gracious living, expect to see the sort of person that you would hope to see marrying your President's daughter up there, otherwise he can't be acceptably the son of a Duke in the play. And that was something that certainly hadn't occurred to us.

RB It's something that brings us up against the fact that Shakespeare is a code-word — a boss-word, perhaps, but a code-word — that in each country designates a certain set of values and expectations. And finding a way through this barrier to the reality that was originally discerned by Shakespeare is always hard.

PB I think that on the one hand the material is so rich that one can say that if you take even a corner of it you're doing pretty well. So one can well understand how in Poland, Brazil, anywhere — where anybody looking at these plays is bound to get ninety per cent of them all wrong because of the translations they've got, not knowing what they're really about — someone will suddenly say, 'Ah, we could do *Much Ado* as a comment on what's happening in Chile at this moment.' And they do it. Well, good luck to it, every interpretation if it works in its place and its moment has some life. But I think that into that totally permissive view, that everything is possible, one can introduce a certain scale of values. One can ask whether the act of interpretation takes the smallest or the widest view of what the play contains. For instance, if in Poland today you see in *Macbeth* something extremely close to the Polish situation, and in doing this interpretation you impose it so firmly that, however much it works, you rob the play of all its ambiguities, you may be doing a successful performance, but you are cutting off your own nose and tying your hands behind your back, because you are at the same time diminishing the play unnecessarily. If you can do the double process, which is to say, 'my interest in this play today is clearly political, but that doesn't blind me to the fact that the play is also anti-political and contradictory and metaphysical. Therefore I won't, because I'm not interested in other aspects of the play, pretend they don't exist' — then most likely I'll discover something and the group will discover something and the audience will discover something. But if I *use* the play, the permissive attitude is at its worst. Because the play is then no longer a vehicle for a re-exploration of truth, it becomes a vehicle for exploitation.

RB Can I take up the word you used, 'diminishing', and ask you to apply it to the problems of costume, or more broadly the metaphoric vehicle for the production as a whole, like the Watteau *Love's Labour's Lost*. Do you think nowadays that a Renaissance costume — which is able inherently to contain many meanings and which denies very little, I would have thought — is the best, or are you prepared to find your metaphoric vehicle in costume terms in any point of history?

PB There are two stages in that. The first stage, literally, is whether or not you're working in the proscenium theatre. For instance, when we did *A Midsummer Night's Dream*, we did several performances of it outside. There was one performance when we took the whole company from Stratford to London and played in the Roundhouse. And we left everything behind — scenery, costumes — and played in our ordinary working clothes. And what was appropriate in one would not have been appropriate in the other. But when you're on anything resembling a proscenium stage, or in that sort of relationship with an audience, when a bank of people are looking at something displayed in front of them, a costume has a quite different meaning from what we've been doing for the last three years, going round Africa and other places. You put down a carpet in the open air and a few hundred people gather round and watch, and whatever you happen to be wearing is a part of life, as in the Elizabethan theatre. It's a quite different thing. So it's a two-stage question. I think the aim, the necessity is that anything visual in a Shakespearean production should not confine the audience to a single attitude and a single interpretation. That's why I think any complete and consistent set of historical costumes is a fantastic imposition, and forces the play in certain directions. Nothing brought this out more strongly than all the work we did on *Lear*. It's quite obvious that all periods are inappropriate — but equally the Elizabethan. I've seen an Elizabethan/Renaissance costume *Lear*; it isn't natural. Take as a yardstick the uninformed audience — and we want the very bright but uninformed audience, with no prejudices, as the yardstick — who's interested if it's interesting, and not otherwise. If he comes and he sees a lot of Renaissance people, that's a fantastically specific statement that's being made to him. And if your aim is to make a reality re-emerge, then you don't make a sort of comment in parenthesis, this was written in a certain period; it's irrelevant. While you're watching the play you want to be in connection with the living element that's unfolding, and you don't want to be reminded of anything that's extraneous to this. There have been many attempts made by political groups – they do this in the German theatre quite a lot – which is to say that the proper Marxist way to look at a play is constantly to be kept aware of the play as something emerging from a certain date in history, a certain time, and to keep all these factors before us, trying to force you to keep that sort of alienation. I saw recently a play directed in this manner, so that for two-and-a-half hours you were always conscious of the play as an example of writing at such-and-such a moment of history. Of course, it's intolerable. You cannot enter into a play if part of you is squashed into that footnoting attitude, you cannot enter into the experience. Now, I think that in a very different way any set of costumes that is self-consistent will have this effect. That's why I think that it's an endless question. I don't know the answer, except that each production will try to come back to it and re-open it. But I think that a mixture of any sort is already a better solution than one that is consistent. And the moment anything is all of a piece, then it's putting a strait-jacket on to Shakespeare.

The other day, we did something that would interest you very much. We filmed for two days experiments with Shakespeare, for French television, in a ruined theatre. It was an absolute ruin, with no stage, a great pit – it was rather like a dump that we were working in. We did a scene from *Coriolanus*, we did a bit of *Hamlet*, a bit of *The Tempest*, a bit of *Romeo and Juliet*, and it was absolutely thrilling to see people in just their ordinary working clothes sitting in a pile of dust, and paving stones, broken stones and rubble, doing the first scene of *Coriolanus*, their imaginations totally released by this. It was very visual, highly evocative. But the visual elements were making provocations to the imagination, not set statements. To put it very simply: the trap is to make statements and to make illustrations. And this is close to thinking that Shakespeare himself was making statements and making illustrations. If we recognise the danger of both, and that he wasn't doing that, we can then discern the other world of vibrations, provocations, and radiating points.

RB The trap may be convention in the widest sense. I'm thinking of the fact that I've several times seen eclectically costumed productions of comedies, which have worked very well – I think of William Gaskill's *A Chaste Maid in Cheapside* at the Royal Court some years back. But I've never seen a tragedy played eclectically. Perhaps there is an inner expectation that tragedy, or serious drama, ought to be consistently costumed.

PB But you saw the *Lear*, in the theatre?

RB Yes.

PB Because in the theatre, there was no consistency, although it appeared to be, because there the eclecticism was not in different styles, but in the fact that we mixed together complete and sketchy costumes. So most of the characters had almost neutral costumes, but key characters had specific and detailed ones. This was a psychological trick that gave an impression of a single world, but in fact being in a way completely eclectic.

RB My recollection is of a complete stylistic unity.

PB Yes, but that was an impression, because in fact we stripped almost everything inessential. One has to be undistracted; a wide eclecticism is distracting, it's busy. You constantly note it in a comedy, you notice all those things, you can't not notice them. And the tragic form of that needs to be as free, but much more invisible, so that you don't notice it.

RB Yes. It's the underlying assumption of jest, of making fantasy about a comedy that permits one the licence to go for the provocations that you speak of.

PB But you know, an example of this is that I've found many times that if today you want an actor in either a tragedy or a comedy to look natural — natural in the sense that you accept him — you just watch him and look at his face and his hands and you listen to what he's saying, and yet you don't want him to look contemporary — almost always you find that the best way of clothing him is to put him in some form of trousers. And you'll find that in many, many productions designers and costume-makers instinctively do something which in photographs fifty years from now will stand out as being so ridiculously characteristic of our time. But for us, men's legs in stockings and breeches have a desperately period flavour. There are many ways of cheating in period costumes, like for instance Lear's servants. If we dressed Lear's servants in any of those horrendous primitivy little skirts and thongs around their legs, you would never have looked at anything else and you could never have believed in their reality. Actually, the actor wouldn't have been able to believe in it himself. We put him in something that looked like a simple garment,but was actually a sort of painter's smock and trousers and boots. The trick is that nobody analyses this and thinks, what are they doing in trousers? Trousers are as natural and invisible today, as in Arab countries a robe would be. Tomorrow, we must think again — but the truth of any given production is only for the people who are actually witnessing it.

RB To move on to another aspect of the matter: what are your views about cutting nowadays. Let's say, the text that you receive that you begin to work on.

PB Well, again I think that in a way we're getting the same answer on every single point. It is with a double attitude, and that is respect on the one hand and disrespect on the other. And the dialectic between the two is what it's all about. If you go solely on one or the other way, you lose the possibility of capturing the truth. I think that the plays are not written with the same degree of finish, it's not in their nature. And some plays are looser and some plays are tighter. In the *Midsummer Night's Dream* I didn't have the least wish to cut a word, to cut or transpose anything, for the simple reason that it seemed to me an absolutely perfect play. In giving oneself the respect for it as something you don't pull around, you then have a much greater chance of getting into its depths, setting yourself the absolute conviction that each word is there because it has to be. Otherwise, to go back to your word 'vibrations', certain vibrations won't take place; but by total belief in the text you find its rightness. Alan Howard played over two or three years with an ever-greater sense of secret meanings he found for himself. In the play, on many levels, endlessly discovered and re-discovered, meanings came from him, that made vibrations passing through Theseus into Oberon and back again across the whole play. And the play was at its best when the whole cast was at a point of high attunement, so that within the performance those vibrations went across it. It's like those sculptures made out of tight wires making a complex pattern, where if the wires aren't tight you don't get the pattern. So that with the *Dream* — although I can well imagine being very entertained by somebody taking a totally iconoclastic view, and turning it upside-down — I'm certain that in enjoying and laughing at and going along with such a production, I would find it less than, a diminishing of, the play itself, where I don't think you can move a word. I think that in other plays you can move words and scenes, but you have to do it in full recognition of how dangerous it is. And I think that this is really something for which there are no rules except the rules of sensitivity, that what in one line doesn't really matter, in another line matters like hell.

RB I think we've come back to a redefinition of the word that you quoted Orson Welles as saying, that we 'betray' Shakespeare, and I wondered about that word, because it seemed to me that it stated by implication an ideal or ethic of loyalty, to which we ought to adhere, and which alas we are not observing. And I wondered how this could be formulated. But in talking as you do about sensitivity and respect, one is perhaps getting as near to the ideal of 'loyalty', if that is the

word that one wants to choose, that describes one's feelings for Shakespeare. So could I ask you finally now, how you'd like to state your
relationship to what we call 'Shakespeare'?

PB Yes, very simply. I don't have any sense of or interest in history
as a reality. History is to me a way of looking at things, and not one
that interests me very much. What I'm much more interested in is
that, in the present, and I mean each person's present, wherever he is,
and whenever it takes place, he and we are constantly betraying reality,
which we don't succeed in perceiving, grasping, and living, and we're
continually diminishing and reducing it. This is the way that we live
through our lives and live in our present, because however we live the
present it's always a highly diminished view of the present moment as
it might be. It's always been broadly recognised that what's been considered as the artist's vision is never a vision turned on the past or the
future, but is a greater possibility of seeing what is actually happening
than the duller vision with which we live through our everyday lives.
This function has been partly taken over by drugs, and drugs have to
a degree once again shown the present in a different light from the
everyday, which is why they have such enormous appeal. But my
interest in any form of art is nothing to do with culture; that doesn't
mean anything to me, either. What interests me is that there are channels
through which we can come into contact for a limited time with a
more intense reality, with heightened perceptions. Therefore Shakespeare to me doesn't belong to the past. If his material is real, it is
real now.

To me, it's like coal. One knows, if one wants to go into it, the
whole process of the primeval forest and how it goes down into the
ground and one can trace the history of coal; but the meaningfulness of
a piece of coal to us today, or anywhere, starts and finishes with it in
combustion, giving out the light and heat that we want. And that to
me is Shakespeare. Shakespeare is a piece of coal that is inert. I can
write books and give public lectures about where this coal comes
from — but I'm really interested in coal on a cold evening, when I need
to be warm and I put it on the fire and it becomes itself. Then it
re-lives its virtue.

Now take this one step further: I think that today the understanding
of what perception is is beginning to change very greatly, and one's
beginning to recognise that the human faculty of apprehension is not
static, but is a second-for-second re-defining of what it sees. Look at
those visual conundrums where you don't know if something is upside-
down — you know, black and white squares that seem to be jumping

inside out. You can actually see how the mind copes with something which is trying to re-understand, trying to verify whether it's upside-down or not. The mind is constantly trying to re-make a coherent world out of such provocations. Now to me the total works of Shakespeare are like a very, very complete set of codes, and these codes, cipher for cipher, set off in us, stir in us, vibrations and impulses which we immediately try to make coherent and understandable. If we enter whole-heartedly into this relation, then all the steps of understanding and reincarnating are steps towards making a world in the present tense, in the present moment, whose only virtues are the standards of meaningfulness, significance, coherence, depth, and one could say reality, truth, as perceived: and that nothing else comes into it. Now within that, because of the completeness of the picture, it can't be simplified in many ways, so that there are archaic elements that are part of it. There are many complex, archaic things that I look at as coming not from history but as something which stirs up in me at this moment my own corner of responses to archaism, which is a very different thing. And so I have to take account of it. What I'm interested to see is not the historical sense but the actual, what makes a meaning for me. And it was through that channel that we eventually, for instance in the *Dream*, came to say: what does magic, what does fairy magic actually mean as a reality within the two hours that you're in the theatre? Not as a convention, but as something which still has a reality. Maybe with completely different outer forms. The word 'fairy' suggests a lot of things, it suggests dead associations. Far behind, it also suggests very living values. If I can touch them, then the coal is burning now.

APPENDIX

The staging of *Timon of Athens* at the Théâtre des Bouffes-du-Nord, Paris

Peter Brook's *Timon of Athens* at the Bouffes-du-Nord gathers up the themes of this book, and presents them in striking and exemplary style. It is undoubtedly the most important Shakespeare production seen in the West in recent years. For us, it is best judged in the categories of the three cardinal decisions described in the Introduction.

(i)   *The choice of play.* *Timon of Athens* is one of the least-played dramas in the canon. I know of no really successful revival anywhere in its attenuated stage history. The choice of this play — which is the first Brook has presented to the public at large since his *A Midsummer Night's Dream* — is at first sight paradoxical, even perverse. Yet the logic of it is dictated by the times themselves. Brook has made this clear in an interview shortly before the opening night, and quoted in the programme:

> Simplement il y a des moments où certains thèmes sont plus proches de nous. C'est ce qui fait que dans certains pays et à certaines époques on joue plutôt certaines pièces que d'autres. *Timon* aujourd'hui est une pièce de pleine actualité: elle traite de l'argent et de l'inflation. Bien sûr ce n'est que l'un de ses thèmes, puisqu'aucune pièce de Shakespeare n'est axée sur un seul sujet. Mais le gaspillage, le crédit, la consommation, les prix et l'abondance y sont présents. Elle met donc le doigt sur des problèmes qui nous touchent. L'histoire de Timon est celle d'un homme qui, en vivant au-dessus de ses moyens, croit acheter la joie. Il se crée un univers — une sorte de paradis — qui n'a rien à voir avec celui dans lequel il vit.

There it is: money and inflation, expressed in waste, credit, consumption, prices and abundance. It is at once clear that Brook sees Timon as a man for our times, a man who tries to create happiness for himself in living above his means. And Timon's reactions to his difficulties are again representative. Brook spells out the topicality:

> il y a donc dans cette ville un homme qui au lieu d'affronter la

131

crise, en étouffe les bruits et crée des mirages. Exactement comme aujourd'hui la plupart des pays occidentaux en face du problème du pétrole : ils font la sourde oreille, continuent de consommer chaque jour davantage, et agissent comme si l'illusion pouvait durer éternellement.

The production, then, is based not on analogies of person (Julius Caesar equals Mussolini, and so on) but profound analogies of situation. There is a central allusion via Timon to the situation of the Western world today. The play is not forced into a tract, but the relevance is there. And it is clear that this production of *Timon* could not have been conceived, or mounted, prior to October 1973.

(ii)   *The text.* The text is a new translation into French by Jean-Claude Carrière, carried out in co-operation with Peter Brook. Brook has explained that he wished to avoid the problems of archaic language that Shakespeare in English inevitably entails for English-speaking audiences. (He has abandoned as a false trail a projected version of *King Lear* in modern English by Ted Hughes.) The new French version is supple, intelligently accurate, and aimed at creating something of the 'mot rayonnant' quality of the original in the linear, hierarchic structures of French. It is in prose: there is no attempt at paralleling blank verse with alexandrines. The style is modern, and it is worth noting that M. Carrière is one of Buñuel's scriptwriters. The text as published has very few, minor, cuts and gives no indication of scene divisions and stage directions. Brook, viewing these as editorial interpolations anyway, presents a text which has the fluidity and the speed of the production itself.

(iii)   *The metaphoric vehicle.* For once, we have to begin with the theatre itself. The Bouffes-du-Nord is a gutted nineteenth-century theatre, only very partially restored. The upper tiers remain, rather precariously: on the ground, half the space is given over to the players, the rest to the audience sitting on wooden benches. There is no formal gap between audience and players, and no footlights. Behind the players is a blank concrete wall, blotched and pockmarked with metal. Thus the audience views (in some discomfort) from what is left of its nineteenth-century inheritance, an action projected against a bleak reminder of the present — and future. The total setting, then, is itself a metaphor for Brook's harsh fable.

The production insists on the verities of the setting. The actors make their entrances and exits through what is left of the decayed machinery of the old stage. There is full light throughout (and no special lighting effects); nothing is done to soften the bleak realities of the house. The actors' dress is eclectic. Timon himself (played by the young and handsome M. François Marthouret) wears a white suit straight from the best tailors of Paris or New York: he is clearly a member of the *jeunesse dorée*. Others wear djellabahs together with homburgs and umbrellas. The Painter wears a symbolic Bohemian neckerchief. The essential principle is that no one locale should be prescribed – the actors' dress reaches out in many directions to suggest a multiplicity of possibilities.

Among the special features of the production, two are worth particular comment. The first is the presence of certain oriental touches. The djellabahs apart, it is an Arab woman whose call, from a high balcony, summons the guests to Timon's first feast. The feast is an oriental affair: there are cushions on the floor for the guests, and the entertainers perform an Arab dance, to Arab music. While there is nothing so vulgar as a direct analogue here, it is a fact that Arab culture is a presence in the production. It enters into the consciousness of the audience, and one is naturally led to make one's own connections concerning the origins of Timon's feast.

The second feature is that of the players to whom Brook gives especial emphasis. Two stand out with much greater force than the text would lead one to expect. Apemantus is played by a black actor, dressed in the style of an Algerian labourer (say) from the poorer quarters of Marseilles. He implies a kind of Third World critique of Timon's frivolity and extravagance; and to the last he has no time for Timon's (equally self-indulgent, as he sees it) railings. Alcibiades' part is projected with great force: he, ultimately, is the symbol of the military *coup* which is the only resolution to the decadence and corruption of Athens. At the last Alcibiades, in dark blue dress uniform with a red cloak thrown over one shoulder, stands against the bare concrete of the back wall to deliver his final appraisal of the situation:

> Conduisez-moi dans votre ville. J'userai de l'épée et de la branche d'olivier. Je ferai que la guerre enfante la paix, que la paix bride la guerre, que l'une soit prescrite à l'autre comme sang-sue et vice versa.

He turns smartly at 'et vice versa'. 'Tambours, frappez,' and he strides down the steps, away from the audience. It is a haunting final image to Brook's fable for our times.

INDEX TO SHAKESPEARE PLAYS